Seumas MacManus

Through the turf smoke

the love, lore and laughter of old Ireland

Seumas MacManus

Through the turf smoke

the love, lore and laughter of old Ireland

ISBN/EAN: 9783744740920

Printed in Europe, USA, Canada, Australia, Japan

Cover: Foto ©ninafisch / pixelio.de

More available books at **www.hansebooks.com**

Through the Turf Smoke

THE LOVE, LORE, AND LAUGHTER, OF OLD IRELAND

BY

SEUMAS MAC MANUS
("MAC")
AUTHOR OF "'TWAS IN DHROLL DONEGAL,"
"THE LEADIN' ROAD TO DONEGAL," ETC.

NEW YORK
DOUBLEDAY & McCLURE CO.
1899

To
ETHNA CARBERY

*Your fond heart throbbed for our country's
  story,
Your great heart glowed for our
  country's glory:
Because it was so, O Banbha's
  daughter,
My tribute take o'er the
  far, far, water.*

To My American Readers:

TRAGEDY and pathos *go leor* there are in our lives, toilsome struggle and patient suffering; but when we gather around the turf fire—old and young, boys and girls—Care slips like a cloak from our shoulders, the oldest is for the hour a child, gaiety crowds the cabin, and merriment fills all hearts. The wand of wit is laid upon us: the joke, the banter, and the merry story, pass; and the folk-tale, old as the babble of our streams, and still as fresh and sweet, is listened to by ears that hearken for the hundredth time as fondly as they did for the first. Alike, grey old pows and yellow little curly locks shake in sympathy for the sorrows of the hero, and wag with delight for his devilment and drollery. The same hearts that rang out a little peal of childish laughter beneath a smoke-blacked Irish roof-tree, have, afterwards, on red fields, often raised a *rann* that fluttered the folds of the defiant and triumphant flag.

In my remote and mountain-barred Donegal, the people, for a niggard living, strive with a surly sea and wrestle with a stubborn soil; they are poor as paupers and hospitable as millionaires. But the wit, the imagination, the poetry, the virtues, the soul, of the most miserable amongst them the wealth of Crœsus couldn't purchase. Civilization (with its good and its ills) has not yet quite felt itself at home amongst us; books are few; so, there, the shanachy, the teller of tales and the singer of songs, still gathers in his old time glory; on long winter nights the world comes and seats itself, spell-bound, at his feet. From early childhood I, with my little tribute of admiration, sat by his feet. The glory of him dazzled me, and I dreamt of one day faring forth and conquering worlds for myself.

—I was a child, I said, and dreamt dreams.

MAC.

NEW YORK, *Oichdhe Brighde*, 1899.

Contents

	PAGE
THE LEADIN' ROAD TO DONEGAL	1
THE BOYNE WATER	21
THE QUAD-DHROOP-EDS	45
THE PRINCE OF WALES' OWN DONEGAL MILITIA	65
BARNEY RODDY'S PENANCE	89
DINNY MONAGHAN'S LAST KEG	113
BILLY BAXTER	141
THE COUNSELLOR	167
THE MASTHER AND THE BOCCA FADH	189
FATHER DAN AND FIDDLERS FOUR	211
JACK WHO WAS THE ASHYPET	231
JACK AND THE LORD HIGH MAYOR	251

The Leadin' Road to Donegal

The Leadin' Road to Donegal*

'TWAS this was the way—
Thady Rooney was a tailyer be trade, and Molly Maguire was as purty a hand at the spinnin' wheel as ye'd meet in the five parishes. Thady was a clane, stout, sthrappin', fine, ecktive fellow, and as daicent as his father afore him—and that's sayin' a dale for him. Molly was a brave, sonsy, likely lassy, that knew how to get the blind side of the boys, and as clane-stepped a *gissach* as thripped to Mass on a Sunday. Now, Thady was on the lookout for a bit of a naybour's daughter that would be shootable to take care of him; and Molly—well, throgs, Molly had no sort of objections to takin' care of a naybour's son, purvided she got one to her likin'. So, as might be expected, Thady

* The skeleton of this tale is traditional, and to be met with in many parts of the North of Ireland, applied to various towns.

yocked,* and he put his *comether* on Molly, and Molly, she blarneyed Thady to his heart's content, till the end of it was—as was nath'ral—they both marrid an' settled down, to stick to one another for betther or worse, through fair an' through foul. An' Thady, who was as industhrus a man as ivir laid down his two hands, set to work, an' he built as tight an' snug a bit of a cabin as ye'd maybe ax to see, jist on a bit of waste ground at a cross-roads where five roads met, and himself and Molly moved intil it; an' Thady went on with his tailyerin', and Molly with her spinnin', and him whistlin' and her singin'—with wee inthervals of love-makin'—as merry as the larks and as happy as the day was long. And for nearly twelve months that pair was held up as a moral for the counthry for miles about, and it was a delight to pass by their door and listen to their light-heartedness. In all that time an awk'ard word nivir crossed the lips of the one or the other of them. But, as ill-luck would have it, the divil—for it was no other—tempted them to agree one night that they

* Began.

could do worse nor buy a slip of a pig. Which of them was so misfortunate as to intherduce the subject I can't tell, but anyhow the bit of a sucker pig was bought and fetched home, an' a snug wee bed of nice, clane, oat sthraw Molly spread for it in the one corner in the tother end of the house from their own bed. And that night Thady had a bad dhraim. He dhraimt that the goose an' the lap-boord, afther doin' a couple of very lively hornpipes an' a single reel on the floor, sat down on the bed to make love, plantin' themselves right atop of his stomach. And with that he wakened up, and be the powdhers of war, what does he find lyin' across him on the bed but the sucker pig!

"Husthee! husthee!" says Thady, givin' the pig a couple of smart slaps that sent it skurryin' an' gruntin' away to its own corner again.

"Molly," says Thady, "I seen pigs in me day with more modesty than that wee pig of ours."

"Arrah, Thady," says Molly, says she, "sure what great wit could ye be afther expectin' of the lakes of it, the crathur? Sure, it's what it felt lonely, jist lake a Christian would, an' hearin' you snorin' as ye know ye do, Thady, in yer sleep, the crathur come up to ye, thinkin' it was maybe its mother was in it."

"Well, I'm sure, Molly," says Thady, "that I feel ondher a mighty great favour to it intirely for the compliment it done me; but all the same, mother or no mother, I'd thank it to keep its distance, and know its place for the time to come."

Well, that fared well till the nixt night wore round, an' Thady had the very self-same oncommon, wondherful dhraim about the lap-boord and the goose; and wakenin' up lake the night afore, there was me brave sucker pig settlin' himself for a sleep atop of Thady, as much at home as an alderman in an aisy-chair!

"Husthee! husthee! Molly Maguire, I'm sorry to say that sucker pig of yours has very small manners."

"Arrah, Thady Rooney," says Molly, "can't ye not be reflectin' on the bit of an orphan pig, that isn't come to the time of day to have sinse? Maybe, Thady avourneen, whin ye were lake it yerself, ye might put yer manners in yer weskit pocket, and no one miss them much."

"No odds for that, Molly Maguire," says Thady. "Ye mind the ould copy-book headline that said, 'Too much familiarity breeds contimpt,' and I considher that sucker pig is pushin' his familiarit⁀ on me rather farther than I wish for. I put corrackshin on him on'y last night for the same dhirty action, and I thought it was a lesson to him, but it saims he can't take a hint onless ye impress it on him, with a stout stick; an' throth, Molly, an' I'm tellin' it to ye now, if I have to dhraw me hand over him again, he'll know what it's for."

"Faith, Thady Rooney," says Molly, "it's well it becomes ye to talk that way of the poor baste that didn't know, no more than that bed-post there, what ye were layin' the corrackshin on it for. If the crathur only gets time it'll gather sense yet."

"That's all very good, Molly," says Thady, "but if *I* don't corrackt it I'm sure *you*'ll not, and a nice pig we'll make of it then, won't we, without breedin' or daicency; it'll scandalise us over the parish, that's what it'll do. If it has a mind to pick up sense it had betther be quick about it, or my patience 'ill wear out, and I'll be tempted to do somethin' that 'ill make it regret it didn't pick itself up in time."

Well, as they say in the stories, that fared well that night again, and it didn't fare ill, and the nixt night wore round. And me bould Thady dhraimt the very same dhraim that third night again, and he bounced up in the bed, tumblin' the pig off ontil the floor, and it run away gruntin' to its corner.

"Great Goghendies! but it's me's the sufferin' man," says Thady. "Molly Maguire," says he, "*get up and put breedin' on yer pig!*"

"Nobbut, Thady Rooney," says Molly, "get *you* up and put breedin' on *your own* pig!"

"Ye lie!" says Thady.

"Thanky, Misther Rooney," says Molly, "it's only a well-wisher would tell me my faults."

The Leadin' Road to Donegal 9

"The pig's none of mine, or he'd know betther," says Thady.

"The pig *is* yours, and so signs on him, he's as conthrairy as his masther," says Molly.

"Throth, then, if I'm conthrairy," says Thady, "I could blow me breath on them smit me."

"Maybe, then, that same wouldn't be coveted, for it was the ill day for some people when yer onlucky breath come about them first."

"I wish to the Lord them people had thought that twelve months ago! If they had, I could have been a happy man this night, an' own for a wife the pick of the parish, instead of bein' the miserable divil I am, with the ugly, good-for-nothin' cross-grained spitfire of a woman that the priest makes me call me own now," says Thady.

"Well, Thady Rooney, *I* wish to the Lord the same!" says Molly. "An' as regards yer bein' a miserable divil, I agree with ye there, too. No one ivir accused Thady Rooney, or one belonging to him, of bein' anything else all their lives but miserable divils—an' miserable, *lazy* divils, too. About the pick of the parish—ye got that—ivery one give in ye got that—and sure it was the nine days' wondher how such a miserable, spavined, ill-formed, yallow rickle of skin and bone, with a countenance as forbiddin' as ould Nick's himself, with a hump on his back and a halt in his step, and his two eyes watchin' each other like murdher across his snub nose, for fear one of them would be afther takin' the advantage of the other—sure I say it was the nine days' wondher what the dickens she could see in ye that made her take ye, barrin' it was bekase she knew ye would be so safe on her hands that no one but the divil would think of runnin' away with ye, and even him atself would be only too glad to fetch ye back as not worth yer room. And throth, I may tell ye, that that same nine days' wondher to them has been a nine months' wondher to me, an' if the divil curses me with ye much longer, I'm misdoubtin' me but the wondher 'ill wear me out me life."

"Ay, there she goes now," says Thady,

The Leadin' Road to Donegal

"there she goes. Jist set her tongue agoin', and Boneyparty himself, at the head of all his rajiments, couldn't stop it."

"Faix, and it's no wondher, for it's sorely fetched out of me, when I have a skin-flint such as you to dale with," says Molly. "But at the same time, maybe I could hould me tongue with you, Thady Rooney."

"I doubt it, Molly Maguire," says Thady, says he.

"Do ye, throgs?" says Molly.

"I do, medam," says Thady.

"Well and good then," says Molly. "I'll thry ye out for it; and let it be that the first spaiks a word, bad, good, or ondifferent, 'ill have to mind the pig."

"Done," says Thady, and he slaps his knee.

Well, be the hokey, that was the quandharry. The conthrariness begun to work Molly, an' up she bounces, though it wasn't more nor the middle of the night, and puttin' on a good rousin, blazin' fire, and boilin' as sthrong a dhrap of tay as iver come out of the black pandy, to rise her heart, she sits herself down to her spinnin' wheel and starts spinnin', at the same time humming "The Geese in the Bog," this way*—

at such a rate that Thady, poor man, might as well think of sleeping in a beeskep. But Thady wasn't going to allow himself to be aggerivated into spaiking so aisy as that. So up me brave Thady jumps, and afther a pitcher of tay that was enough to lift a man's heart up through the riggin', he crosses his legs on the table, and dhrawin' a pair of half-finished trousers that he was doin' for Father Luke to him, he stharts sewing the trousers and whistlin' "The Black Joke," lake this—

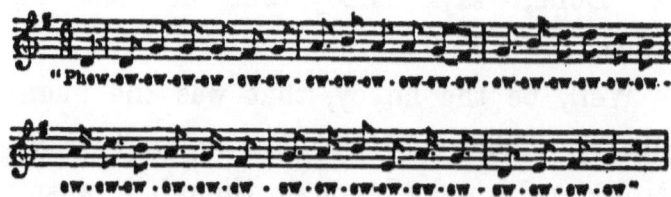

And there the two of them pegged away, and lilted and whistled away like a pair of thrushes; and, if ye'd believe their purtend-

* To be as effective as intended, parts of this story must be acted rather than read.

in', ye wouldn't know which of them had the lightest heart. And whin Molly, the crathur, got tired of " The Geese in the Bog," she started on " Larry O'Gaff," and Thady, poor man, whistled up " Go to the divil and shake yerself" with a vingince that was enough to loosen any woman's tongue. But Molly was good grit, and she only spun harder and put more life into the lilt. And things went on this way till in the coorse of a little time a pony and thrap dhruv up till the door with a jintleman and his sarvint in it. The jintleman was makin' the best of his way for the town of Dinnygal, and bein' a stranger in them parts, and not knowin' the right road when he came to the cross, and seein' the light in the wee cabin, he pulls up his pony, and says he to his sarvint, says he,—

" Go intil that house and ax them if they'd kindly diract ye the leadin' road to Dinnygal."

So the sarvint lifts the latch of the door, and ye'll be afther believin' he opened his eyes purty wide when he seen Molly spinnin' and liltin', and Thady sewin' and whistlin' with as much unconsarn as if it was twelve o'clock in the day with them.

"God save all here," says he. "Isn't this the purty night entirely?"

Molly lifted her head and looked at him, and then went on with her spinnin' and hummin,' and Thady lifted his head and looked at him, and then went on with his sewin' and whistlin' again, but naither of them said *dhirum* or *dharum*.

The sarvint was a trifle mismoved at this, but he walked up closer to Thady, who was now whistlin' "The girl I left behind me," and he says, says he,—

"It's benighted we are, meself and the masther without, and we'd feel obligated to ye if ye'd kindly put us on the leadin' road to Dinnygal."

Thady wint on with his work unconsarned, and says,—

says Thady, says he, comin' down hard on the last bar or so, an'—without ivir movin' his eyes off his work—timin' it with three or four shakes of the head in the dirackshin of Molly, as much as to say, "Ax her, and she'll tell ye."

Then the sarvint turned to Molly, and says he,—

"Prosper the work, good woman, and could ye oblige meself and the man without be puttin' us on the leadin' road to Dinnygal?"

Me brave Molly was spinnin' away and hummin' away at "There's nae gude luck about the house," and she wint on with her work, but makes answer,—

says Molly, says she, hummin' away, an' without liftin' *her* eyes off *her* work, only—jist like Thady—comin' down hard on the last bar or two, and timin' it with three or four shakes of *her* head in the dirackshin of Thady, as much as to say, "Jist let his lordship himself tell ye."

Faix, at this the poor man made for the door, as if there was a rajiment at his heels, and goin' up to his masther says,—

"We'd betther be takin' the first road come handiest to get out of this, for it's a branch office of the asylum for oncurable lunatics, is that cabin there."

"Get out, ye omadhaun," says the jintleman. "Did ye not make out the leadin' road to Dinnygal?" says he.

"No, I made out the leadin' road to the door," says the sarvint, "thanks be to Providince for his marcy; and it was the speed of me heels carried me out of it. I seen mad men and mad weemen," says he, "in me time, but the lake of what's goin' on in thondher I nivir rested me eyes on afore and trust I nivir may again."

"Confound ye for a numskull," says the jintleman, jumpin' down and throwin' the sarvint the reins. "Hould them things till I find out the road."

"God bliss ye and send ye safe back," says the sarvint, as the jintleman wint in of the door.

The jintleman marched up to Thady, who was sewin' away and whistlin' away without ivir liftin' his head, and, says he,—

"Could ye tell me, good man," says he,

The Leadin' Road to Donegal 17

"or give me the dirackshins of the leadin' road to Dinnygal?"

Thady went on with his work, and replied,—

"Phew-ew - ew-ew - ew-ew - ew - ew - ew - ew - ew-ew - ew - ew-ew - ew"

says Thady, says he, indycatin' him for to ax Molly as afore.

Then the jintleman wint up to Molly, who was as busy at her work as what Thady was at his.

"Prosper the work, good woman," says he, "and could ye dirackt me on the leadin' road to Dinnygal?"

Molly nivir lifted her head, but answers him,—

"Him - im-im-im-im - im-im-im-im - im - im - im-im - im"

says Molly, says she, sendin' him back the same way to Thady for information.

And there he was in the quandharry.

"Ah, be this and be that," says he to himself at last, "I'll bait the biggest button on

2

my coat that I make ye spake, ye ould haythin', ye," says he to himself, refarrin' to Thady.

So with that he thurns to Molly again, and says,—

"Well, in throth, me good woman, ye mightn't be ashamed to open that purty little mouth o' yours to reply to a sthranger, for—though it's afore yer face I say it—I'd thravel far afore I'd see another mouth as coaxin'," says he.

says Molly, says she, back to him, but this time she did look up from her work, throwin' the most soothcrin', deludhrin', coaxin', sly look at him sideways, an' noddin' her head to him on the last notes, mainin', "Throth, ye spake thrue there, good man, but how do ye lake me now?"

"I think, good man," says he, then, thurning to Thady—"I think, good man," says he, " ye would hardly refuse a sthranger jist the laste little taste of a kiss from that purty little wife o' yours," says he.

The Leadin' Road to Donegal 19

"Phew-ew-ew-ew-ew - ew - ew-ew - ew - ew - ew - ew-ew - ew - ew-ew - ew - ew"

says Thady, says he, gettin' as black in the countenance as a thurf, an' shakin' his fist three times on the last notes, right in the sthranger's face.

"Now, what do ye say to that yerself, me purty little woman?" says the jintleman, thurnin' to Molly.

"Hm - hm - hm-hm-hm - hm-hm-hm - hm - hm-hm - hm-hm - hm"

says Molly, says she, givin' him another of her sootherin' looks, an' waggin' him on with three wags of her forefinger an' her head, as *she* come out with the last notes.

"Oh, ye natarnal hussy, ye, I knew it was in ye," says Thady, jumpin' off the boord in a thundherin' rage.

"All right, Thady," says Molly, says she, jumpin' up and clappin' her hands with delight. "All right, Thady," says she, "You MIND THE PIG!"

The Boyne Water

The Boyne Water

WILLIAM SCOTT and Liz'anne were not accounted exemplary citizens in our little republic of Knockagar. Very far from it. Independent of the civil feuds which disturbed the Scott household, they were hardened sinners against society at large in that they never visited either church or chapel— the unpardonable sin with us. Though the young people, the waggish, and the less serious-minded, enjoyed William and Liz'anne, their irreligious conduct continually kept all the gray pows in the parish shaking.

William's own father and mother had been of different religious persuasions, and they had spent their life squabbling over whether William should be a Catholic or a Protestant, with the result that, though William earned his father's grudge and his mother's goodwill by lustily professing himself "a thrue Roman," he practised no religion.

It might well have been thought that, with the unhappy results of a mixed marriage so vividly before his eyes, William would steer clear of the danger. But, as Donal a-Thoorisk said, mixed marriages, like wooden legs, ran in the blood. William, noisy Catholic as he always was, began early to show a partiality for the daughters of the Heretic, and, to nobody's surprise, wound up by a runaway marriage with Liz'anne, whose own people immediately cut her off.

But all things considered, William made a promising start. He had succeeded in inducing Liz'anne to submit to a Roman Catholic marriage. At this there were many optimists among us, willing to suspend judgment till we'd see further. But again many others would not take a roseate view of matters. They prophetically said, "You'll see what you'll see!" then closed their mouths hard, and shook their heads. And, I regret to say, events justified this prophecy.

For six months William and Liz'anne got on agreeably as well as comfortably. William was a weaver, and famed for good workmanship. And Liz'anne was as good, as tidy, and as clean a housekeeper as any of the most religious women at the Bocht. When she had her house trigged up for the day, and she had sat down in the front window to her sprigging, while William worked the loom close by the back window, and two spotlessly white cats—for Liz'anne was fond of cats and always kept two big ones—sitting on their haunches on either side of the swept hearth dreamily dropped their eyelids, and purred at each other across the fire, it was a pleasure to go into William's and have a chair, and be soothed with the comfort that filled the cabin. For six months, William and Liz'anne kept their religious opinions under due restraint, and their happy content was uninterrupted. There was no danger of dispute about going to church or chapel, for neither of the pair had any decided *penchant* for visiting either.

Now William was not a drinking man in the usual acceptation of the term; he had no craving for drink, but he seemed to feel that he owed himself and society the duty of getting gloriously drunk two or three times a year. And when William got drunk, his religious enthusiasm came uppermost, all the religious sentiment that had accumulated in his soul since he was previously on the spree suddenly began to boil, and William, quite indifferent to the religious susceptibilities of neighbours of a different way of thinking, threw open the safety-valve, when any who didn't choose to get out of the way were welcome to their scalding. William was now rampantly and aggressively Catholic, eager to let his blood colour the sod in the cause of his beloved Faith. His antithesis was Orange Watty—a weaver likewise—who lived under Dhrimanerry hill, not far distant. And hither, when the religious outburst seized him, was William wont to betake himself, creating a hostile demonstration in front of poor Watty Farrell's: "Whoop! Hurroo! To *** with King William, an' God bliss the Pope!"

Watty Farrell was spare and small of frame; he had a short temper, and was an ardent, fiery Orangeman, who gloried in being standard-bearer on "the Great Twelfth," and defiantly flaunted the flag in the face of the exasperated enemy—although, "the Twelfth" being past and no other burning religious feeling being in the air, his Catholic neighbours had not a more cordial or a more esteemed friend than Orange Watty. Let Watty, though, be in what frame of mind he might, the instant he heard William Scott's defiant voice raised without, blaspheming his idol, and invoking a blessing on Anti-Christ, he bounded from his loom, all the Orange valour within him surging through his blood, and insignificant as he was in size, it always gave his big burly sister, Bella, enough ado to hold in her clasp his squirming form, until by some means or other she had got the door barred and bolted, and the danger of little Watty going out to commit homicide thus considerably lessened. And when William, waxing yet more insolent, sang loudly,

>Wor ye iver in Glenties fair ?
>>Says the Shan Van Vocht.
>Wor ye iver in Glenties fair ?
>>Says the Shan Van Vocht.
>Wor ye iver in Glenties fair,
>Where (HURROO!) they clip the Orange mare,
>And make stockin's of her hair ?
>>Says the Shan Van Vocht,

Watty, like a caged tiger, screamed and raged within—and felt anything but soothed when William added him of a good stomachful of personal abuse, ere he left.

About six months after his marriage with Liz'anne, William let himself out on one of these royal sprees, and went through his usual programme, including the customary visit to Watty's and outpouring of bile thereat. But, as the fates would have it, big Bella being from home, and so no restraint upon Watty, the little fellow had come out, and—for William was too drunk for defence—"hammered the papish sowl-case out of him"—so Watty eloquently described it, after—and chased him for his life!

When William came home after his ignominious defeat at the hands of such a miserable little *droich* as Orange Watty, he was not in the sweetest temper—and the animus he bore King William was much intensified. He tried to steady himself in the middle of the floor, and to look the haughty papist to perfection. He fixed his gaze on Liz'anne, who, in the window-seat, sprigged away industriously—"To (hic) *** with him, I say! To (hic) *** with him! To (hic—hic) *** with King Bi(hic)-Bil-hilly!" That was too much for Liz'anne's militant Protestantism to tolerate. She got up instantly, and to the utter consternation of the already well-abused William, seized a creepy-stool and whacked him out of his own house. " Now, to *** with yerself, an' the Pope, an' with every dhirty papish from Connaught to Guinealand! an' a necklace o' red-hot mill-stones roun' yer necks to keep yez there when yez are down!" and the justly indignant Liz'anne, casting a last contemptuous look at her poor amazed husband where he sat on the street vaguely feeling for his sores, slammed out, and bolted, the door. And when at length William felt collected enough to gather himself together, he stood a good while gazing at the inhospitable door, which coldly stared him back; then he shook his head with grievous meaning, and turning away felt it very hard that, owning a house, and a comfortable one, he was compelled to go and petition the Bummadier (the village pensioner) for the favour of a night's lodging.

It took ten days probably for William and Liz'anne to consent to forget this, their first little disagreement. But it remembered them that they had each a faith to defend, and henceforward they were slow to let pass without doing their duty any opportunity offered. Of course I do not mean that they attended to the outward observances their religions required of them—they were not guilty of going to church and chapel, nor did they commit themselves to prayer, any more than formerly, but they were henceforth staunch advocates of their respective faiths, and waxed great in polemics.

"Well, for the life o' me," on a day when polemics raged, William would say from his seat at the loom, "I can't tell for what did they curse me with the name they did! *William!* Och, to *** with it! Hard feedin' to them, an' my left-handed blissin' be on them done it!"

"Ha! ha!" Liz'anne would sarcastically laugh, throwing back her head. "No more do I know why they give such a name to the lakes (like) o' ye. Hard feedin' to them, say I, an' conshumin' to them! an' *my* left-handed blissin' be on them lakewise!" Liz'-anne was very bitter, and in debate had that sort of a triumphant crow with her, which exasperates.

"It's a name for a jackass," William would angrily retort.

"If that's so, they fitted ye well. But I say it's Pathrick you should have been called —that's the proper name for a jackass."

"Houl' yer tongue, ye barge ye!" and William would stamp his foot. "Ye varago ye, houl' yer tongue!—If ye can," he would add, tauntingly.

"Yis, Pathrick it should 'a' been," and Liz'anne would calmly move about her work, "for any jackass called other than Pathrick is miscalled."

"Sent Pathrick was a jintleman, ye targer ye! What you, or wan belongin' to ye, nivir was, nor niver 'ill be. Don't dar' for to even a word again' Sent Pathrick!"

"Make yer min' aisy—I wouldn't soil me spoon on him if I met him in the stirabout pot."

"Ha-ha-ha! Yez haven't got the lakes of him any how among yer haratics."

"Ha! ha! In throth an' if I thought they suffered the lakes of him among them, I'd turn Turk the morra."

"Ho, ye natarnal vag ye! Ye would, would ye? Faith an' the Thurks, if they knew ye as well as I do, would prefer yer room to yer company. An' didn't I tell ye hundreds o' times not for to go for to abuse Sent Pathrick—don't do it!"

"Then don't you be throwin' the dhirty spalpeen in my face."

"Oh Lord! Oh Lord!" poor William would exclaim in agony.

"The dhirty spalpeen, indeed!" Liz'anne would repeat, seeing the sore spot.

"Ye *will* dhrive me mad, woman! Oh, Lord!"

"Hagh! ye've put that out o' me power—for it's long since ye went mad. I niver met that papish yet hadn't the mad touch in him. What did they disgrace the good an' holy name of King William puttin' it on you for, anyhow?"

"It's me was disgraced by gettin' it."

"Get out, ye papish beggar! Don't say it!"

The Boyne Water

"Hagh! ye Orange tar-maj-ent ye, I'm disgraced."

"Ha! ha! disgraced! The divil himself couldn't disgrace you—no more nor soot might disgrace a chimbley-sweep."

"Ma'am, ye're goin' too far. Ye'd temp' the Pope."

"The Pope, *moryah!* To the divil with you an' the Pope. The Pope! Och, short daith to *him!* If I owned a pig I had any respect for I wouldn't let *him* carry *broc* (refuse) to it."

"Oh Lord! Lord! Will ye let the Holy Pope alone atself that's not intherfairin' with ye!"

"An' didn't I tell ye afore to keep yer ill company to yerself? If ye don't want him abused don't go for to be throwin' the vagabone in my face."

"Vagabone! The Holy Pope o' Rome! Marcy look down on us! Are ye not afeerd, woman? Are ye not thrimblin'?"

"Och then the divil a thrimble's ailin' me, I thank you."

"Vagabone! Vagabone! I'll tell ye what it is, me good woman, if, be hook or be crook, them words o' yours reached him, there'd be an ass's head on ye in five minutes time!"

"Ha, ha, ha, ha! An ass's head, indeed! An' throth I'm afeerd there's too few of his own sort could spare the wan he'd give me. An ass's head! Ha, ha, ha!"

Poor William wasn't nimble-witted enough for the sarcastic Liz'anne. He never entered into argument with her that he, somehow or other, didn't come out second best, for she could, metaphorically, twist him around her finger, and cast him over her shoulder with an ease that was gall to William's soul. To William's credit, be it said, no matter how much she enraged him, he never dreamt of physical force as a good argumentative agent.

Of course these theological disputes were not perpetual. Very far from that. A day or two of each month might be set apart for them; during the remainder of the month, Liz'anne was a dutiful wife and William a loving husband, and to all appearance, whilst they consented to forget their religions both enjoyed more happiness and content than could easily be expected of such unregenerate ones.

When a young generation of Scotts were growing up, additional causes of disagreement entered into the lives of William and Liz'anne. There might, indeed, have arisen serious difference of opinion over the baptising of the children only that William, who, when he saw a material advantage could be thereby gained, was possessed of a share of policy, and taking the easy way of Liz'anne—the *only* way in which she could be thwarted—had them christened as he desired. True, on the occasion of her first, the Bocca Fadh* (with William's connivance) gave it a hurried private baptism—intending thus to have the foreway of Liz'anne if with returning strength of body should come stubbornness of mind. But the moment he had finished the snatch-ceremony in William's kitchen, it would be difficult to say whether his pain or his amazement was the greater at the stout blow that took him over the head, and set a squadron of stars doing intricate evolutions before his eyes, for Liz'-

* Long Beggarman.

anne, in her bed in the room, suspected something, and arriving on the scene robed in a manner not quite appropriate to the kitchen, and for which the exigency of the occasion was her excuse, had seized hold of Shan a-Phiopa's (who had come to the christening) stick, laid on the Bocca Fadh with a precision and effectiveness of stroke very creditable indeed for a woman whom the conventionalities of society require to be hovering between death and life. Anyhow, on this occasion there was more of life than death dealing with Mistress Scott's arm and tongue, for she very quickly cleared the Bocca Fadh out of the house, loaded with a sore load of both physical and moral abuse— and the other trembling revellers who had assembled to enjoy the christening had gratitude in their hearts when she let them escape with a tongue-thrashing. The Bocca Fadh paraded his wounds around the parish, and made much capital from a humble comparison of himself with those good and renowned men of the early church who were martyred in the same cause in which he had so sorely suffered.

But a time came, and the neighbours told William it was a shame that he wasn't sending the children out to chapel; and it forced itself on William that it was part of his duty, as a good Catholic, to do so. He wove for them some of his best tweeds, and John Burns carefully took the measure of the eldest, and, making necessary allowances for variation in size, cut out the making of nice suits for all of them after this standard. Liz'anne found what was going on; she didn't say much, but began making little necessaries for them, also, resolved they should go to church. As the day of the children's *debut* approached relations became strained, the tension gradually increased, and, on the eventful morning both William and Liz'anne joined in dressing the children, vieing which should do most, and heartily abusing each other's religion all the time. But, alas! William was faultlessly dressed himself and sporting his Sunday shoes on which Liz'anne had, the night before, bestowed a magnificent polish—and so prepared to go *with* the children. Here he had poor Liz'anne, whose wardrobe—neat and clean and plentiful enough for housewear—boasted no holiday garments. Eventually, when she had with infinite pains fitted the children up in their neatest, and saw that William stood by the door waiting to guard the flock into the proper fold, she lost at once her resolve and her temper; she huddled the children out of the door, pitched poor William out on top of them, "Here, an' away to *** now, you an' them!" she said, and slammed the door.

But, of their five children, Liz'anne won to her church the allegiance of four. The fifth and eldest hoisted William's colours, and was very proud to proclaim himself "a jiggered papish." Religious disagreements were now no less rife. But William had long since tired of the monotony of being beaten, and had given up trying on such occasions to return Liz'anne word for word, and he schooled the son who had shown himself worthy of him, to express his feelings rather by looks than words—though he himself still employed words. When, occasionally, a religious difference would now arise, William without any delay laid down what he styled the Boyne Wather, a shaft of alderwood about twenty feet long, which from the hearth passed down the centre of the floor, dividing the house equally. When the Boyne Wather was laid down it was a mutually understood and respected rule that Liz'-anne and her following were to keep to the front half of the kitchen, while William and his small but staunch support kept the other half. Insulting words and looks flung across the Boyne Wather were of course quite within the rules of war, but on none but the most urgent account could either party trespass on hostile territory—whereby this Boyne Wather surpassed its original. The waggish ones of the Bocht, who took a sinful delight in the religious controversies which troubled the lives of William and Liz'anne, were fond of quizzing the former when they got him at wake or other gathering where fun was the order.

"Well, William, is the Boyne Wather down or up, this weather?" and the interrogator, with a twinkling eye, appealed to the humour of the house.

"Och it's down, down," with a mournful shake of the head. "I had to fetch it from behind the house" (the customary resting place of the Boyne Wather when peace reigned) "yistherday evenin', an' glory be to Goodness!" with a sigh, "it's down yet, an' small signs of thon woman lettin' me take it up."

When William had got the Boyne Water safely laid, and got to his loom again amid a hail of abuse from Liz'anne, he wrought harder than was his wont, and he made the shuttle fly to an unending accompaniment of "No wondher! No wondher! No wondher! No wondher!" his sole, and very exasperating reply, now, to Liz'anne's abusive arguments. As long as Liz'anne continued bestowing hurtful epithets on William and William's church, so long would William, in a doleful voice, continue the Jeremiad—"No wondher! No wondher! No wondher!" thus stinging Liz'anne into protracting her unedifying discourse, which, by reaction, lengthened in turn William's mournful chant. And let happen what domestic events might, or let who would come in or go out, whilst the Boyne Wather was down, and the fit on William, he went on with his loom and his plaint, the shuttle swinging to and fro, his head nodding to it in a mournful manner, and he proclaiming " No wondher! No wondher! No wondher! No wondher! No wondher!"

On a Twelfth of July William's second son, who had been honouring the occasion not wisely but too well, came swaggering up through the Bocht, eliciting from the echoes lusty cheers for the pious, glorious, and immortal King William, and right heartily and boisterously abusing all the enemies of the said William and of his church. The William who had fallen away from the traditions of his name, to wit, the enthusiast's own father, heard him with deep mortification, and slunk in a convenient door till the son who shamed him had passed. He felt called upon to apologize for the conduct of his unworthy offspring; he shook his head dejectedly—" I don't know how that is," poor William said, " for that boy comes of wan of the d——d best Catholic stocks in Dinnygal!"

The children of William and Liz'anne disappointed us all—pleasingly disappointed us —by the good turn-out they made, for we had ever had our forebodings about their future. They went to America one by one, prospered, and never forgot the old couple.

When the children had disappeared the Boyne Wather began to be requisitioned less often. Very probably it had got to be laid down on Patrick's Day and the Twelfth of July—but William and Liz'anne would be more than human if this wasn't so. During the remainder of the year it lay behind the house in merited neglect. It was not that either had got any less zealous in their religion. William remained, what always he had been, one of the staunchest Catholics that never attended chapel—and Liz'anne, in like manner, and to the like extent tendered unabated loyalty to her church. But old Time had softened the asperities of both tongue and temper, and strengthened that regard for each other, which, despite their disputes, William and Liz'anne had ever maintained. For years it had been a standing joke for the countryside, how, Watty Farrell having once happened into William's when the Boyne Wather was down and the wordy artillery in full play across it, and having had the temerity to join Liz'anne in her abuse of William, Saint Patrick, and the Pope, Liz'anne had without more ado emptied a bucket of water over the audacious little weaver, and then emptied him, dripping, out of the house.

And when William got "the sthroke"* and every one thought him dying, Liz'anne, despite the bitter, sleety, awful night it was, dashed out, unshawled and unhooded, and off to Father Dan's at the top of her speed, and, not finding Father Dan at home, ran again, breathless, four sore Irish miles to Corameenlusky where he was attending Hughy Shan's old mother, and carried him off with her, to give to William the consolations of his religion. And William received these as hopefully as many a more regular Catholic.

William lingered for several weeks, and Liz'anne's concern and attentions were touching. For all of that morning upon which he died, William kept repeating one word—"Liz'anne, Liz'anne, Liz'anne, Liz'anne," as unceasingly and persistently as he

* Paralysis.

44 Through the Turf Smoke

had ever chanted "No wondher! No wondher! No wondher!" over his loom. It was the ravin' of death, they said, was on him. Despite the heart-whole prayers of the good old women of the Bocht, assembled in his room beseeching God to give him a happy and sudden release, William's dying moments were protracted. It was at length agreed that the presence of a heretic was the cause. The weeping Liz'anne, poor woman, agreeing with this opinion, quitted it, and, according to expectation, William soon closed his eyes in peace.

The Boyne Wather was laid down, for the last time, at William's wake—but this time across the hearth, making several very warm and cheery fires for the comfort of the wakers. They all knew its history, yet the boys who had so often made merry about it, joked not on the occasion.

The Quad-dhroop-eds

The Quad-dhroop-eds

A TRUE TALE OF THE CRUCKAGAR DEATH
OR GLORY DEVOTED SONS OF WILLIAM
L.O.L. 19,019.

THE Cruckagar Death or Glory Devoted Sons of William L.O.L., 19,019, had long been a shining light amongst the Loyal Orange Lodges of the North. The burning eloquence of the rhetoric that from it flowed and the dazzling brilliancy of the brave and dauntless deeds the Death or Glory Boys threatened to perform if only opportunity offered, marked them and their lodge as the worthiest inheritors to whom had descended the glorious traditions of stubborn fights and bloody fields, the heritage of Aughrim and the Boyne.

The Cruckagar Death or Glory Devoted Sons of William L.O.L., 19,019, had been, we said, the shining light amongst its sister lodges. But alas and alas, that we have to relate it! that light which shone so long, so brightly, and so steadily, the Pole Star of all who worshipped at the shrine of Civil and Religious Freedom and Equality, and detested Pope and Popery, Base Bigotry, Brass Money and Wooden Shoes—alas and alas! that light was, to the extreme concern of all true, peaceful, and law-abiding subjects—subjects whose excess of loyalty and burning love of law and order prompted them to kick even her Most Gracious Majesty's Crown into the Boyne if she obeyed not their mandates—that light, again we repeat, was eventually dimmed and finally obscured forever.

And in this way the lamentable catastrophe came about.

One of the fundamental rules of the Cruckagar Death or Glory Devoted Sons of William L.O.L., 19,019, was that the toast of "The glorious pious and immortal memory" of William who freed us from the neck-collar of Rome and the wooden shoes and other impositions of France, might be pledged as frequently as the members chose during the first half-dozen toasts, but for a very good reason, gathered from experience, was not to be attempted after the sixth round. This wise ordinance was strictly and piously observed till the cloak of Worshipful Grand Master fell upon the shoulders of Billy M'Carter, one of the most militant members of a most militant lodge, and certainly one of the most sincerely devoted children that ever worshipped the memory of his illustrious namesake of the Boyne. Billy's unmasterable, unrestrainable enthusiasm prompted him to toast his regal namesake's memory first of the toasts, and second of the toasts, and then third of them, fourth of them, fifth of them, sixth of them, and seventh of them; the eighth toast was to the memory of William, as were likewise the ninth and tenth. The intelligent reader has, of course, foreseen the result, and the reason why the children of William, as children of many other parents, disputed, disagreed, separated, and the lustre of family records was dimmed. Yes, about, or after, the sixth toast, Mister M'Carter's voice lost its distinctness of utterance, with the alarming result that henceforward he was toasting "The glorious pies (hic), and immor'al mem'ry" of King William! And finding the martial-spirited Billy unamenable to reason, Murray M'Clure led the revolt. The adhesion to his side of the Rev. Simon M'Whan, too, intensified matters, and swelled the numbers of the rebels. The more ardent spirits among them stood fast and firm by their Worshipful Grand Master and the lodge. The excitement was great. Informal meetings of both parties took place nightly, the Rev. Simon M'Whan harbouring the insurgents. Active hostilities were quickly instituted, and the great guns of both parties were wrought to bursting, hurling deadly discharges of rhetoric across the way at the encampment of the enemy, and evoking as thundering, as death-dealing, volleys in return. Both sides had submitted their case to the higher authorities with the least possible delay, each claiming for itself to be the True Devoted Sons of William. The higher authorities found themselves unable to decide the delicate and complicated question, and referred it back to the claimants for mutual settlement. But the breach was now too wide, and their respective principles had, ere this, burned themselves into the breasts of either party. Billy hurled Anathema at Murray and Simon. Murray and Simon hurled deepest and direst Anathema at Billy.

And lo, the excitement in Cruckagar got a new impetus! On a morning Billy M'Carter astonished Cruckagar by producing a sympathetic letter from no less famous, no less renowned a brother of the most zealous and prominent brethren of the North, than the great William Aughrim Roarin'-Meg. Walker, Governor of the Apprentice Boys, Worshipful Grand Master of the Londonderry Glorious Memories of Bloody Fields L.O.L., 99,942, stating his opinion that Mister M'Carter was a worthy sufferer in the good cause, that he and his faithful followers were undoubtedly the True and the only True, Sons of William; that they reflected honour upon their Order, glory upon the Cause, and renown upon Ireland, and that furthermore, he, William Aughrim Roarin'-Meg Walker, Governor of the Apprentice Boys, and Worshipful Grand Master of the Londonderry Glorious Memories of Bloody Fields L.O.L., 99,942, should take an early opportunity of going down to Cruckagar to strengthen the hands of Mister M'Carter, and make his unworthy enemies humble them in the dust before him!

There was joy in Israel! In Gath was wailing and weeping and gnashing of teeth!

II.

Paddy Monaghan's "Bush" was richly deserving of its intended title of Omnibus. Its uses were, indeed, varied and manifold. There was a happy appropriateness in Masther Whorisky's expressed opinion that Paddy's Bush was "a versatile arrangement." The Bush had been superannuated at the Major's, when Paddy got it for the taking away. Then in the summer time Paddy had it brushed up and ornamented, when it answered alike to drive a child to be christened, or a pair to be married, or—an "impromptu hearse" the Masther put it—a corpse to the grave. One day it drove out a party of merry pleasure seekers, next day a group of wailing mourners. On Sunday it drove the Major to church, and on Monday it took "a crathur in the faiver (God save us all!)" to the hospital; on Tuesday it took the sheriff to the courthouse, and on Wednesday it took poteen to Donegal; on Thursday the magistrate sat in it; on Friday it had a load of eggs and butter, and it finished up the week by going to the town for drunken Mat, trundling him home and dropping him at his own door. Then, in the winter time, when trade was dull, Paddy's Bush made a most admirable combination dog kennel and fowl house; for, whilst Mrs. Monaghan's roosters and three turkeys perched on the rack above, and the ducks, with one grey goose—the others were stole from Shusie, good woman, at Hallowday by the card players, bad luck to them—squatted under the seats, the terrier and the brown colley slept comfortably on the cushions. Yes, it *was* a versatile arrangement.

On a certain day Paddy's Bush trundled to Londonderry with a (very) general cargo. It was fair day in Londonderry. When Paddy had discharged the cargo he took a stroll through the fair. There were on view, in addition to the other animals common at fairs, horses, mules, jennets, and quaddhroop-eds—a quad-dhroop-ed being Paddy's nomenclature for what the practical man who now reads these pages would simply and straightforwardly call a jackass.

Now Paddy bethought him that as the Ware-day was on him he required, as in previous years, a quad-dhroop-ed for the purpose of back-loading manure up to the broken ground in the nor'-aist park, and consequently, prices being suitable, a quad-dhroop-ed he bought. Then the question arose how was he to get it home. He searched the fair, but didn't find a man from the neighbourhood of Cruckagar who might lead the quad-dhroop-ed home for him. What was he to do? He consulted with Aaron M'Clay, for Aaron, now a Derry merchant, hailed from Cruckagar, and still took a lively interest in his native place, and a friendly interest in any person therefrom. Paddy Monaghan was a particular favourite with him, for Paddy carried him the weekly budget of doings and sayings at Cruckagar. Paddy, we say, in his perplexity, consulted with his friend Aaron; and his friend Aaron suggested why not take it home in the coach? The idea was a good one. Paddy had neither parcel nor passenger to take back, barrin' a new skillet for Nancy, Father Dan's housekeeper, to boil Father Dan's spuds in, and a new Dolly Varden hat for Kitty Shinaghan, of Sheskin, that was trying to catch Pat the Widower, that intended takin' another wife, they were sayin', afore Lent; and easily he could carry these items on top of the coach, lodging the quad-dhroop-ed inside, and pulling down the blinds, so that man or mortial wouldn't know whether it was the Sheriff of the county or the Lord Lieutenant himself, was within. A bright idea it was. So with Aaron's help, in Aaron's yard, quietly and quickly, the quad-dhroop-ed was coerced into the Bush, the blinds drawn, and the door fastened; and Paddy Monaghan started on his return journey. No sooner did Aaron see him safely off than he went to the Post Office, and—for he was a wag, and moreover owed one to Billy M'Carter—telegramed to Seshaballymore office, the telegram office nearest Cruckagar, that William Aughrim Roarin'-Meg Walker, Governor of the Apprentice Boys, and Worshipful Master of the Londonderry Glorious Memories of Bloody Fields L.O.L., 99,942, had taken his departure from Londonderry *en route* to Cruckagar, and that he would arrive at his destination at or after 11 p.m. in Mr. Patrick Monaghan's coach, and it was to be hoped that Mr. M'Carter and Mr. M'Carter's friends would give him a royal Donegal welcome!

The Postmaster at Seshaballymore was a loyal Orangeman, was a warm friend and partisan of Billy M'Carter's, moreover. So, an equestrian messenger he despatched—Jimmy the Post—on the Dapple, with the good news to Billy. Then was the *furor* in Cruckagar, and the rush and the push, and the scouting and scurrying, till the great news was dispersed to the extremities of the parish, and the copy of the telegram itself went round, the fiery cross to bid Billy M'Carter's legions in. And by half-past ten o'clock that night there wasn't a true Orangeman within the bounds of the parish who still owned allegiance to Billy and his cause, that didn't stand on the street of Cruckagar with colours displayed awaiting the bold Billy's behest. Band and banner were quickly paraded to head the procession, and torches being lighted and music struck up, a gallant body of not less than three hundred brave and dauntless brethren of the Cruckagar Death or Glory Devoted Sons of William, L.O.L., 19,019, marched gallantly forward on the Derry road.

Three miles out, Paddy Monaghan's Bush was sighted, trundling along the moonlit road. A wild cheer rent the air, the band quickly struck up "See! the Conquering Hero Comes," and rapidly they advanced. Paddy was looking behind him, surmising to himself who might be coming after, that they were going out to meet, when he found the Bush surrounded by the hoarsely howling excited multitude, his mare unloosed from the vehicle, himself unceremoniously hauled from his seat and hustled aside. He endeavoured to ask two or three, by shouting into their ears at the top of his voice, what it all meant; but even if he could shout loud enough to make himself intelligible in the midst of the deafening cheers that continuously rolled up, no one had time to listen to him, much less answer his questions. In another minute, six Death or Glory Devoted

Sons of William, getting within the shafts, had started the Bush, and the triumphal procession, leaving Paddy and his old mare a dumbfounded, not to say ill-used, pair. Though from thence to Cruckagar the drummer drummed, and the fifers fifed for all they were worth, they drummed and fifed in vain, for volley on volley of cheering unintermittent, drowned their drumming and their fifing as completely as though they had only made a pretence to drum and fife. Into Cruckagar the procession rolled, gathering volume as it went, and through Cruckagar and up to the door of their lodge, which stood right opposite the Rectory, in which they were quickly made aware the Rev. Simon with Murray M'Clure, and their partisans, had assembled to sympathise with each other, and to watch the proceedings opposite. Right in front of the Rectory parlour window, where the base ones and the deserters could, to their gall, get a full view of the proceedings, the six Death or Glory Devoted Sons of William within the shafts of the Bush rested from their labours by command of Billy, and three ringing, defiant cheers were given which, like daggers, pierced the very souls of the M'Clurites within the Rectory. William Aughrim Roarin'-Meg Walker, who had not hitherto —as indeed became one so illustrious among his people—chosen to acknowledge the ovation in his honour, nor yet even drawn the blinds, would now, on opening the door of the Bush, and ere yet he had stepped down from it, be asked to stand full front towards the shrinking foe (in the Rectory), and there with scathing tongue lash the treacherous ones till they writhed again! Joy of joys to Billy, the moment of sweet retribution long looked forward to, was now at hand!

But there was still a slight, unaccountable delay. The blinds were still undrawn, the door of the Bush unopened. Surely the occupant had not, could not, have fallen asleep, nor yet remained asleep during the proceedings of the past half-hour, proceedings which might have called the dead out of the graveyard? Billy knocked a respectful knock at the door of the Bush. A painful pause. "Three cheers for Misther Walker an' King William." With all the power of their lungs this was responded to. Billy knocked again. Another painful pause. "Three cheers for Darry walls." This demand, too, was well and loudly honoured. Billy gave a third knock—a bold one this time. During the pause, now, a batch of eager faces were discerned pressed against the panes of the Rectory parlour window. "Three more cheers, boys, for Simon an' his sarpints." Responded to with enthusiastic venom. There was nothing for it now but to open the door of the Bush and find what was the matter. Open Billy had it in a jiffey. Yes, there was a noise inside as if of some one gathering himself together for the purpose of emerging. Billy and the crowd fell back a pace at this to give him room, and at a signal from Billy, to greet William Aughrim Roarin'- Meg Walker, Worshipful Grand Master of the Londonderry Glorious Memories of Bloody Fields L.O.L., 99,942, on his emergence, the crowd as one man set up "The Battle of the Boyne":

> "July the First, in Oldbridge town
>   There was a grievous battle,
> Where many a man lay on the ground
>   By cannons that did rattle:
> King James he pitched his tents between "—

And at this instant the inmate of the Bush, from the door projected a head adorned with two enormous lugs, and, jealous that they should have all the music to themselves, forthwith lifted up his voice in one long, loud, and most harrowingly unmelodious bray! Those people who write fiction, finding their imaginations unable to cope with a crisis they have created, have a shallow trick of slinking from their duty by saying, "Here we drop the curtain." Now, willy nilly, I am constrained to make use of the shabby subterfuge of these fellows.

Here I drop the curtain!

III.

Raise it again, and behold it is Sunday morning. And we are in Church—Cruckagar Church, too; for there you see many of our old friends. Billy M'Carter, with melancholy mien is below; Murray M'Clure, with something akin to a gleam of malignant triumph on his face, sits well to the front; the Rev. Simon M'Whan, with a meek expression on *his* face, is just entering the pulpit.

"Dearly beloved," the good man said, adjusting his glasses and taking up the large Bible, "for my text this day you will turn to Numbers, twenty-second chapter, twenty-eighth and twenty-ninth verses—there we read—

"'And the Lord opened the mouth of the ass, and she said: "What have I done to thee? Why strikest thou me, lo, this third time?"

"'Balaam answered: "Because thou hast

deserved it, and hast served me ill: I would I had a sword that I might kill thee." ' "

. . . . .

On the Sunday following, a little flock, with Billy M'Carter as pastor, met for Divine worship in one of Billy's barns, and from that time forward constituted an independent congregation in themselves. As they assumed no name, a name was sought for them, and one for their pastor. Balaam, his enemies gave to Billy, and the Quad-dhroopeds to his congregation. Their first collection, be it noted, was lifted to compensate Paddy Monaghan for a slaughtered animal.

The Prince of Wales' Own
Donegal Militia

The Prince of Wales' Own Donegal Militia

THE P. W. O., or Prince of Wales' Own Donegal Militia, was, in the year of our tale (some fifty years since), one of the finest bodies of men that ever outflanked a beefsteak, or stormed a breakfast-table; whilst the cool and dauntless audacity with which half a dozen of the heroic fellows would attack a solid square of porter bottles, and carry a magazine of beers at the point of the corkscrew, has ever been alike the envy and the admiration of every other body of military in the Green Isle—the famous North Corks not even excepted. True, their enemies urged that in point of discipline they were not quite what would have been expected of a martial body sporting the proud colours of Britain, and that their courage in time of trial would not be of the mould to reflect eternal honour on the proud flag, under whose glorious shadow it was their envious, unpurchasable, etc., privilege to march. But very evidently the malicious grumblers, who would so slander the Prince of Wales' Own, never saw those gallant troops marching to dinner—hay foot, straw foot, right foot, left—or each struggling manfully in the last ditch with his seventeenth bottle, else the lips of the vile slanderers had on those points been sealed *et in secula seculorum*. It must indeed be admitted that in the Prince of Wales' Own Donegal Militia the undue familiarity which, we are told in the proverb, is apt to breed contempt, obtained rather much between the non-commissioned officers and the privates for the three-quarters of the year during which they were gentle and peaceable civilians, waxing their ends, knotting their threads, philosophising at street corners, pedestrianising for—for—health, I suppose, and profit; collecting bric-à-brac and antiques in exchange for pins and needles; bird-fancying—a pleasant and gentle vocation which they usually followed by the silvery light of the horned moon; and the other multifarious *pursuits* in which the soldier-civilian during his long vacation takes a part. As a consequence of the familiarity so begotten, when they donned the uniform they unfortunately did not sink the civilian in the soldier, and the respect paid by the private to his sergeant was in many instances just not such as was due to a military superior. Indeed, if the truth must be told, perhaps the sergeant or the corporal did not always preserve that dignity and *hauteur* towards his subordinates which is usually of necessity affected by men of rank to inspire those beneath them with respect and awe. As—pray listen:

"Number Twinty-wan, will ye hould yer gun crackt—don't think it's a hatchet ye have in yer hand goin' to knock down a pig. Do ye hear me, Dolan?"

"Troth, I do hear ye, Sarjint; it isn't hard to hear ye this wee while; ye make more noise lately than ye used to do *leapin' off the table.*"

A hearty subdued laugh ripples along the line.

"Number Twinty-wan, I'll make it

hot for ye afore ye go home to Susy again."

"No need, Sarjint, avic, makin' it hot for me—it's not a *goose* ye have in it. I'm not frettin' about gettin' back to Susy, aither; I know she can live rightly, for I left plinty of *cabbage* behind for her."

"Ye're a deep scoundhril, Dolan."

"Not as deep as *a tailyer's thimble*, Sarjint."

"I'll thrash the sowl out of ye some day."

"*Baste* it out of me, ye mane?"

"Yer onsobordinate, sir."

"Say that one again, Sarjint; it's a thumper, wherever ye come by it."

Then elsewhere—

"Stand at aise, Three-an'-thirty."

"I am at aise."

"Thurn out yer right toe," curtly.

"That's not yer right toe, ye omadhaun ye; do ye know the toe ye bliss yerself with—the hand, I mane. Thurn out the toe of that hand—the toe of that fut."

"But I don't bliss meself with me fut, Corplar."

"Number Three-an'-thirty, thurn out the right toe of yer right fut immaijetly."

"Have a bit of raison with ye, Corplar Muldoon; sure, haven't I five toes on me right fut, an' I'm blowed if I know which of the five ye want me to thurn out."

"Thurn out yer right fut immaijetly, M'Guiggan, or I'll have ye drum-headed, ye scoundhril."

"There's me right foot out now. I didn't like for you to go an' reflict on me foot by evenin' to me that I had only the one toe on it."

"Hould yer tongue, sir."

"I'll have to let go the gun if I do."

"I'll take the uniform off ye, M'Guiggan."

"Ye couldn't."

"Couldn't I?"

"No, *for ye haven't got yer pins** about ye."

"I'll take the uniform off ye, sir, an' I'll give ye—"

"Twelve rows of pins, at laist; divil a toe

---

* Rag-pickers give rows of pins in exchange for the wares they receive.

it 'ill go into yer bag this day for less, Corplar."

"Ye're a low-lifed scrub, M'Guiggan."

"Thankee, Misther Muldoon; ye can keep that yerself."

Also—

"Shouldher arms!"

"Shouldher arms, Three-score!"

"Sure I am shoulderin' them as fast as I can."

"It takes ye the divil of a long time to do it, then; an' yer as awkward-lookin' at it as a monkey playin' the piano. Numbers Two-score-an'-nineteen, an' Three-score-an'-wan, plaise shouldher arms to show Three-score how to do it with grace. Do ye obsarve that, Three-score?"

"Och, I obsarve it; but do you obsarve that I don't thank aither of them boys to do it with grace. Two-score-an'-nineteen is used at shouldhering his budget; an' Three-score-an'-wan is a butcher, an' sure ye nivir yit knew a butcher that wasn't *graise* from the sole of his head to the crown of his foot—from the crown of his sole, I mane, to the head of—I mane from the foot of his crown to—to— Ye know what I mane."

"Faix, it would be afther takin' a purty smart man to know what you mane—barrin' when yer hungry; ye make people undherstan' that quick enough."

"Ay, Sarjint, avic, it's 'like masther like man,' ye know."

"Shouldher yer arms, sir, and keep that extinsive mouth of yours closed, or I'll be able to see nothing behind it."

"Closed it is, sir; an' I'd always oblige ye by keeping it out of yer light if I could only know when ye're lookin' this way—but that same isn't aisy, troth, from the deuced conthrairy way them purty pair of eyes of yours has of lookin' across aich other."

"I'll have ye removed out of yer ranks, sir, and put undher guard."

"Well, I'll thank Providence an' you for the happy relaise."

It happened on one sunny day in a sunny June of the time heretofore hinted at, that Colonel Bloodanfire, having distinguished guests, resolved to entertain them by a field day and general review of his gallant Donegals. In his cups, on the previous night, he had committed himself to several comprehensive and sweeping statements regarding the discipline and courage of his beloved regiment—statements which, viewed in the cold and searching light of day, rather astonished the gallant colonel himself, presenting as they did a somewhat different aspect from that which they bore when only the red glamour of the wine fell upon them. But Bloodanfire was a man of his word; with him there was no retrospection when once he had put his hand to the plough, or even to the bow—the long one. His character and the character of his regiment were at stake, and he was resolved all should put their best foot foremost—be the same either the foot decorated with the hay-band, or the one ornamented with the straw; for so were his intelligent and courageous fellows ingeniously aided in distinguishing respectively the right foot and the left. Accordingly, a council of war, alike of the commissioned and the non-commissioned officers, was called on the morning of the great, the eventful day, at which the Colonel laid before his subordi-

Prince of Wales' Donegal Militia 75

nates the state of affairs, and urged upon them the pressing need of making on that day a special effort to far excel all their brightest records of the past, and with united will, by a long pull, a strong pull, and a pull all together, at once pull the regiment through the ordeal satisfactorily, and pull him out of his dilemma. By a judicious use of corkscrews, he screwed their courage to the sticking point, and each man became loud, in fact very loud, not to say noisy, in his protestations and declarations of using his every endeavour to make that a red-letter day in the annals of the Prince of Wales' Own Donegal Militia. And they kept their word, only too well.

It was well advanced in the forenoon, almost bordering on the afternoon, when the regiment, which had been under arms all morning, was marched out to an extensive plain a short distance from the Barracks. The Colonel's guests, both ladies and gentlemen, were there to witness the celerity and the extraordinary military talents, of which they had heard so much, of the boasted regiment. The Colonel, informing his friends that this was his strong point, kept his men for some hours marching and countermarching, forming and wheeling; and going through again and again the elementary drill, which they did with *éclat*. At least the Colonel said it was with *éclat;* an enemy to the Colonel, and to the fair fame of this gallant body of men, who happened to be on the ground, however, said that *éclat* must in that case be French for *noise*. The Colonel had, so far, been nervously endeavouring to stave off, as far as possible, the event of the day, a sham battle between two sections of his men, the probable result of which he could only anticipate with fear and trembling; and he thought if he could only keep it back, the sky might fall, or the earth open, or fire and brimstone come down and consume the whole dodgasted concern, anything, anything—he was careless and reckless as to their mode of final and complete extinction—only let them be annihilated somehow, and his credit saved. But, unfortunately, after he had kept off the critical action till his guests had begun to upbraid him with delay, and his stomach to reproach

Prince of Wales' Donegal Militia 77

him with neglect, and his men to grumble audibly, asking to have even a bit of dinner carried out to them in a red handkerchief, for that their bellies were bidding their backs "good-morrow"—after he had thus earned ill-will on all hands, and the fates and elements had successfully failed to perform a diversion on his account, such as he piously prayed for, and both earth and sky still doggedly remained unmoved, he was at length compelled to give the dreaded order for the division of the regiment into two sections, for the purpose of engaging in the bloodless encounter, one section standing motionless to receive and repel the charge of the other. The brave fellows on each side, goaded by the cravings of their stomachs, feeling far more deadly enmity towards the Colonel than towards each other, although about to engage in mortal conflict, now raised their voices in noisy protest against the inhumanity of making them fight on empty stomachs. The battle must go on though. The Colonel determined to meet his fate like a man. A hurried whispering might have been observed going on amongst the Colonel's friends. One of them, a young fellow, with a humorous twinkle in his eye, slipped away, unobserved by the Colonel, and left the field. The two divisions, not indeed very blood-thirsty looking, but porter-and-beer-thirsty enough, faced each other at a respectful distance. The order, so long withheld, was at length given to the attacking party; forward they moved, first at the quick, then at the double quick. Things began to get exciting. The attitude of the approaching columns did now certainly begin to look threatening to those who awaited their attack, with growing trepidation and indecision, in front. Very evidently the oncoming party, being in a bad humour, were resolved to make some one pay the piper; the motionless party saw this and quailed. The space between them was short, and rapidly diminishing; another minute, and the crash would come, and—

Ding! Dong! Ding!

The party to a man came to an instantaneous halt! It was the great dinner-gong whose surprising tones rang out so suddenly and unexpectedly! Now! what—

DING!! DONG!! DING!!

Both parties glanced instinctively towards the Barracks, and then towards each other, and—

DING!!! DONG!!! DING!!!

The imperative tones of that last overcame any little scruples that might have existed in their minds. The order of the dinner-gong was the first order that the Prince of Wales' Own Donegal Militia had learnt to obey with alacrity. However dilatory they may have been in performing other, as simple, manœuvres, that consequent upon the sound of the mid-day gong was picked up and gone through with a readiness and tact which verily astounded the drill-sergeants. Never had the sound of the gong been so welcome to their ears. Would they disobey? Decidedly not! With a " Hip!" " Whoop!" and " Hurroo!" they fled and they sped, helter-skelter, quick and quicker, over ditch and dyke, hedge and fence, without stay or pause, till pell-mell they tumbled into the Barrack-yard, panting and gasping and struggling for breath.

Poor Bloodanfire had to affect joining in

the hearty and rapturous peal of laughter that burst from his friends, and accompanied them to dinner, having nothing else for it. When dinner was over his guests lost no time in urging upon him the necessity of getting out his flying squadron (at whose atrocious breach of discipline he determined to merely wink) once more for the promised encounter. So after they had ravenously devoured their meal, the Prince of Wales' Own Donegal Militia were again marched out for the dread encounter. The Colonel and his friends took up a commanding position on the field, the offensive and defensive ranks faced each other, word was passed along the lines that Colonel Bloodanfire expected every man that day to do his duty. The command was at length given, and the attacking party now started at the double quick. The effects of a hearty dinner and a bottle of porter had produced a reaction, exalting their spirits; so they soon increased their pace to the treble quick, every man of them itching for the chance of lathering the sowl out of an opponent. But their opponents, having to stand cold-bloodedly awaiting the attack, had

Prince of Wales' Donegal Militia 81

not that stimulant to courage which a hot race at an enemy ever begets; on the contrary, they fidgeted and murmured, and what courage they had been possessed of, began to ooze out, like Bob Acres'. The other party neared them; misgivings, many and serious, took hold of them; they looked behind them, looked at the Colonel, finally once more at the oncoming whirlwind, and with one impulse, as one man, they executed a right-about-face movement with a promptitude and expedition that they had seldom exhibited on the parade ground, and *fled!* Yes, they fled, with even a swifter pace than what they had shown in obedience to the dinner-gong. They fled far, far away, over the field, over a crowd of loungers who had come to see the day's sport, over hedge and over ditch, till they had got well out of the battle-field. The Colonel, seeing this, boiled over, his friends got hysterical with laughter; then the Colonel got scarlet, and white, and purple, and black. He swore loudly, and the officers of the retreating division swore loudly in sympathy, and halloed and shouted after their fast retreating forces, who, however, had neither time nor inclination to listen to orders. I intimated that the whole division fled, which was not exactly correct; for one valiant private, Donal M'Glanaghy, Number Two-score-and-five, held his ground dauntlessly like a man and a soldier, and by repelling (with the sole aid of his soldierly bearing) the attacking force, which retreated from the attack in high good humour, thus earned for himself the glory which otherwise had been distributed over half a regiment.

When the flying squadron had been overtaken by their officers, and by the Colonel, who pursued them hotly also, and surrounded and brought back to the field—for the Colonel was determined now to have the manœuvre out, at any cost—and hotly and roundly rated, and their deep disgrace, and the disgrace they had brought upon their regiment and their Colonel, and even their country, in the eyes of the satirical strangers, had been painted to them in very glowing, or —I might plainly say—in red hot, words, by their naturally enraged Colonel, they were told that now, under pain of the severest

Prince of Wales' Donegal Militia 83

penalties court-martial could inflict on them severally, they must receive and repel the attack. The two divisions were again formed, the order given, and the attackers came on a third time.

"Holy Moses!" said one of the defensive party, as the others swiftly approached, "do ye observe the look of mischief in Condy M'Garry's eye?" referring to one of the attacking party.

"Throth an' I do," said a neighbour of the speaker's. "I see a look of murder in his eye; an' the same lad isn't to be thrusted. Be the same token he has the ould spite into you since the night of the *shindy* down at Monaghan's, when ye gave him the nate little bit of a dinge on the skull. Look at the eye he has in his head now; as sure as there's powder in Darry he manes to give ye a knock—look out for yourself!"

"Be the powdhers, then, he'll not have it all for nothing! he'll get the same sauce that he gives, with, maybe, more spices in it. Here's at ye, M'Garry, ye sowl ye! Whirroo!" And he hereupon sprang forward from the ranks to meet the attack, and with clubbed musket levelled the wholly-innocent Condy.

"A-hoo!" "Hip!" "Hurroo!" "Fag-a-ballagh!" That, and not the officers' orders, was the real signal for the attack. There was now some motive to fight for, and some real tangible benefit to accrue from thus fighting, far better than a mock affair in which poor fellows playing at acting on the defensive could only experience dread and uncertainty at the formidable and armed host hurled against them, and who might mean sham or reality just as circumstances would, on the spur of the moment, prompt. Besides, here was an opportunity, a grand opportunity, for them to cover their late disgrace. Providentially, the means of vindicating their fame is thrown in their way, and they must take advantage of it. They hesitated not, but threw themselves at once, with their muskets clubbed, on their opponents, who in their turn entered as warmly and heartily into the spirit of the thing as could be desired. It was utterly useless for the Colonel to go about raging and stamping and swearing, with the officers bawling, and haul-

Prince of Wales' Donegal Militia 85

ing, and pulling, and striking right, left, and centre—all was quite useless. Both sides pitched into each other with a spirit that left not the strangers in a moment's doubt as to whether or not there was courage in the Prince of Wales' Own Donegal Militia. They slashed and smashed, struck, prodded, parried, and crashed, yelled, and shrieked, bellowed, cheered, and hallooed, giving every evidence of being engaged in one of the fiercest encounters witnessed on a European battlefield since memorable Waterloo. And after a long and stiff struggle the "defensive" party drove their attackers clear out of the field, and in a deep ditch beyond they pommelled, till they were tired and wearied, at all who could not succeed in escaping.

On the following morning there was assembled on parade a highly picturesque, motley, and vagrant-looking crew, with the value of a little fortune in sticking-plaster ornamenting their broken features, listening to a severe harangue from a highly-enraged Colonel.

"And now, Number Forty-five," said the Colonel, when he had used up all the threatening, as well as vituperative, language the English tongue vouchsafed; "and now, Number Forty-five, Donal M'Glanaghy," said the Colonel, "kindly step forward."

Donal—the hero who had valiantly held his ground on the previous day at the second attack, when the remainder of his comrades had so disgracefully fled—Donal now stepped forward with one arm in a sling, one eye closed and black, and a ridge of sticking-plaster extending from his nose to his right ear. He raised his sound arm in salute.

"Private Donal M'Glanaghy," said the Colonel, "when your unworthy comrades on yesterday disgraced themselves, their regiment, and me, you alone held your ground in a manner of which I was proud, in a manner which reflected the greatest credit upon your training and upon yourself, and which"—and here the Colonel stamped and threw a fierce look at the dilapidated ranks before him—"and which can not be permitted to go unrewarded. Say what would you wish as a recognition of your sterling manliness."

Donal blushed, touched his cap, and said,—

"Well, yer honour, Colonel, I'm thinkin' maybe ye'd be afther givin' me the Victhory Crass. I b'lieve it's given in reward for such actions."

"What! the Victoria Cross!" said the Colonel, taken aback. "The Victoria Cross! Oh, but you know, my good man, that is an honour only given as the very highest and greatest reward for the most daring and valiant action a British soldier could perform. The Victoria Cross! Oh, no, no, my good man, that is far beyond my power. You will have to ask something else, something more moderate, something more in reason."

"Well, then, Colonel, yer honour," said Donal, touching his cap again and standing erect, "if ye couldn't give me the Victhory Cross, maybe, Colonel, yer honour, YE COULD GIVE ME AN OULD HALF-WORN PAIR O' THROUSERS YE'D HAVE NO MORE USE FOR!"

Barney Roddy's Penance

Barney Roddy's Penance

BARNEY was not naturally bad. Take him in the round, and, I daresay, he had full as many virtues as the average Irishman. But the fact is, he was inveterately addicted to fibbing. Still, his stories were invented with the very laudable object of entertaining his listeners. If Barney could not invite you to his own home, there to help him partake of a good dinner or a warm supper—simply because he had no home—he did the next best thing in his power, and strung a good thumping lie into a rather enjoyable yarn, and then and there treated you to it. I cannot say—I never could find out—whether Barney expected you, in return for his kindness, to put any degree of faith in these yarns. Some held that he did. But, be Barney's wishes what they might on that subject, I am certain that no one ever did believe one of his stories—unless, indeed, it was some innocent stranger whom Barney got into his hands. "It's as thrue as one of Barney Roddy's yarns," passed into a proverb in that part of Donegal which Barney honoured with his residence, and signified that the statement in question was a forty o. p. lie.

"Barney," said I, one evening in harvest —as I took my seat on the whin ditch beside which he was digging potatoes for Mickey Roarty—"Barney, it's a great wonder to me you never married."

"Is it, faix?" And Barney dug on with seemingly increased energy for the space of five minutes, during which time I was careful not to disturb him.

"Is it, faix?" he queried again, as he crossed his arms on the spade and looked me squarely in the face. "Maybe it's me that was married! an' well married, too! Hagh! Ay, it wasn't to *one* I was married at all, but to a dozen of them! To a dozen divils, an' ivery one of them worse nor the other!" saying which he plunged his spade viciously into the ridge, and resumed his digging in a fierce manner.

Barney Roddy's Penance

"What do you mean, Barney?" said I, for I saw that he now only wanted the invitation to commence spinning a yarn; "sure, if you married a dozen you would be transported for polygamy."

"I nivir had anything to say to the girl, thanks be to Providence!"

"Never had anything to say to what girl?"

"Polly Gammer."

"Oh! Barney, you mistake me. Polygamy means the marrying of a great number of wives. How do you mean to say that you could marry a dozen?"

"I don't know if there was a dozen. There was eight of them anyhow, I daresay; but I nivir counted them."

"And what tempted you to marry eight wives?"

"It was pinance for my sins."

"I should say that was a severe penance. I have known men who had only one wife, and they allowed their life was a burthen to them."

"Throth, then, them men's life was a Garden of Aiden compared to mine for the ten days I was in the blissed state of matthermony. I married my wife out of purgathory—St. Pathrick's purgathory*— and I had to take all her sisthers an' aunts, for sivin jinnyrations back into the bargain, an' be me socks I got me fill of them. It was a sevair pinance!"

"Tell me all about it, Barney."

"Give us a *shough* of that pipe. Thanky. Keep yer eye about ye for fear ye'd find Micky Roarty comin', an' give me warnin'; for he's a dhirty bear, an' thinks if he gives a man a shillin' a day with praties an' point, he thinks you should make a black neygar of yerself an' work the very sowl out through yer body for him; if he sees ye liftin' yer head to say 'God save ye' to a naybour passin' the way, ye'd think he'd jump down yer throat." Here Barney seated himself comfortably on a head of cabbage, and puffing the pipe like a steam engine, he commenced.

"Well, to yock at the beginnin', ye see it was the time I lived in Tyrone, afore I come into this counthry, a party of us, naybours,

* Lough Derg.

Barney Roddy's Penance 95

was comin' back from the fair of Dhrimore, an' be the same token, there wasn't a man in the party that wasn't rather gay; an when we come as far as Nancy Hannigan's my throat was as dhry as a lime-burner's hat, an' I said we wouldn't pass it till we'd know what sort of stuff Nancy had in the wee keg. No sooner said nor done. We knocked up Nancy in a gintale way be puttin' in the door with a rock, an' afther Nancy thrated us for our kind attintions, we got into a wee bit of verrins (variance) as regards which of us was the best man. There was a weeny bit of a tailyer, the size of two good thurf an' a clod, an' he got up on the table, whin the argymint was at its highest, an' he commenced abusin' ivery man of the party with langidge a dog wouldn't take off his hands, an' he said if he had only his own lapboord he'd clear the house of ivery mother's sowl of us, while he'd be sayin' Jack Robinson. Troth, the impidence of the wee rascal put us to a stan' for a minute, an' when I got me breath agane, I took the wee brat by the scroof of the neck an' threw him out of the door, an' as he was flyin' out I give him just a nate little nap with me stick that happened to crack his skull. But we did what we could for him—ordhered a nice coffin, an' expended tuppence-ha'penny to have it painted black; give him a rousin' wake; an' then the funeral was somethin' to open yer eyes! We got six other tailyers to carry him on lapboords, an' berred him with a goose at his head. It was more than the wee divil desarved; but seein' that he met with the wee mistake in our company, we thought we would do things square by him, an' we knew the display would be a consolation to his widda. Well, of coorse, I thought it was all over an' past; but what would ye have iv it, but Father Luke kicked up such a shindy over the affair, that he'd almost laive ye ondher the impression there was nivir a man's skull cracked in the North of Irelan' for a hundred years afore. An' it would be enough, too, if it was a *man's* skull that was cracked, and not sich a dawny wee sickly *droich* of a thing. Howan'ivir, the upshot of the whole thing was that Father Luke ordhered me to Lough Dharrig (Derg) to do pinance.

"Well, when the time come round, I spit on me stick, an' made for the Lough. An' maybe I hadn't a high ould time of it there. Pinance! Throgs ye'd niver know what pinance is till ye'd go to Lough Dharrig. The Lord forgive me, it's often when I should be sayin' a mouthful of prayers for the sowl of the wee tailyer, it's often I'm afeard it was inventin' new curses for him I was. Sweet good luck to him if I didn't suffer in Lough Dharrig that tarm for him! Thundher and thumps, I had a corn on my feet fornenst ivery day of the week, an' it's as careful I was about them corns, as I would be about my own mother; but the usage they met in Lough Dharrig, throttin' thim Stations on me bare feet, was enough to dhraw tears from a stone. Ye'd think ivery pebble on the path was spayshally sharpened agane my arrival, an' whin wan of me corns would come down atop of a pebble that had a corner on it as sharp as a fish-hook, I would give a yell, an' jump the height of meself, jist landin' down with another corn atop of the next stone! Between the yellin' and the skippin' I'm thinkin' that ye might put my prayers in yer weskit pocket without much throuble to ye. There was one ould *voteen,* an' he had a skin to the sole of his own foot that was as tough as a donkey's hoof, an' when I jumped, an' yelled, an' come down maybe atop of some of me naybours, he would say—the infarnal scoundhril!—that I was a disgrace to the place, an' that I should be put out. Then, the night I had to sit up in the chapel—och, that was the tarror intirely! Whin I was bobbin' over me head, an' foun' I couldn't houl' out any longer, I said to meself I would jist close me eye for three winks; but the words were scarcely out of me mouth when, by Jimminy! the same ould *voteen* gives me a rap over the skull with a *crosshin* of a stick that I thought he lifted the top of the head clane off me. I thurned on him an' I gave him a look that would split a stone wall. 'It's for the good of yer sowl,' siz he. 'Throth,' siz I, 'it may be for the good of me sowl, but it's not for the good of me crown. An' me good man,' siz I, 'if it was any other place but the groun' ye're in, maybe ye wouldn't be so handy with yer stick. For three fardins,'

Barney Roddy's Penance

siz I, 'I would take it from ye an' give ye the father an' mother of a good soun' blaichin',' siz I, 'ye snivellin', ugly-lookin' scarecrow ye!' But all the norrations I could praich to him wasn't a bit of use; he'd just turn up his eyes lake a duck in thunder, an' no surer would I thry to close an eye agane but he lit on me with his *crosshin;* an' he stuck to me all night, an' no matther what part of the chapel I moved to, to get out of his way, he was at me shouldher agane in a jiffey, with the whites of his eyes thurned on me, an' he waggin' the *crosshin* at me iviry time he caught me eye. Be me socks, my sowl seemed to be of far more consarn to him than his own. Well, in the mornin', glory be to Providence, I had *nallions* on me head the size of yer two fists, an' I swore that if ivir I'd meet the natarnal vagabond outside of the island, I would give the poorhouse carpenther a job on his coffin. The sarra saize me, but I had murdher in me heart! an' little wondher—for me head wasn't sound for three-quarthers of a year afther.

"Howan'ivir, I soon got into betther humour, an' forgot all about me head, bekase I got an intherduction to Nelly Moriarty, a widdy woman, with a snug sittin' down not far from me own townlan' at home. Nelly, as I thought—poor deludhered fool that I was!—Nelly was purty good to look at. She had cheeks as red as fresh-painted cart-wheels, an' ivery other accomplishment accordin' to that. But there's no denyin' it, the three cows' grass that I knew her to have made her look a long sight purtier in my eyes, an' the short an' the long of it was, that afore I left the island I put me *comether* on Nelly, an' afther blarneyin' her up, I puts the word to her, an' faix we settled it all up square.

"Holy St. Pathrick! but I was the oncommon great ass! I thought we'd be as happy as the days were long; an' I said to meself, 'Barney, me boy,' siz I, 'yer jist settled for life; and it's nivir a hand's thurn ye'll have to work more, but jist put yer two hands in yer pockets and go about like a gintleman. Nelly, be coorse,' siz I, 'with her three cows' grass 'ill support ye lake a Prence o' Wales, an' the longest day in summer ye can throw yerself on the back of the hill—on the three cows' grass—an' lie there in the sun, whistlin' jigs agane the larks, an' snappin' yer fingers at the worl' an' the divil.' But och, it's little I knew what was in store for me. An' Nelly Moriarty, it's mistaken I was in you intirely! An' I soon foun' that out when I married into the family. When she fetched me home afther the weddin', the sarra saize me if I could a'most make my way in of the door, for it was crammed from the hearth to the threshel (threshold) with sisthers, an' aunts, an' mothers, an' gran'mothers, an' the divil himself only knows how many other faymale relations, all subsistin' on the three cows' grass! 'Be the hokey,' thinks I to meself, when I seen the congregation—'be the hokey, I'll soon make a scattherment on the nest.' But it was all the other way roun'. For the first week I couldn't complain much, barrin' that I had too many masters; but I didn't grumble much at that yet, for I flatthered meself that I would thurn the tables, as soon as I'd get me footin' made, an' I'd make them go packin' in detachmints. In another week, I sayed to meself, if they didn't stop their jaw, I would show them the hole the mason made—which is the door. But *movrone*, what would ye have of it but poor Barney's plans went *ashaughrin*. Ye see, just to oblige the wife, I used to get up first in the mornin' an' put on the fire for them, an' make the wee drap of tay; an' throth if there had been a bit of rat-poison any way handy I would have sweetened a good many of the bowls with it. But in the coorse of a week, I thought I would commence to show I was masther of the house an' the three cows' grass. So, next mornin', when Nelly hilloes in my ear,—

"'Barney!' siz she.

"'What?' siz I.

"'Are ye awake?' siz she.

"'I'm not,' siz I.

"'Ye're a liar,' siz she.

"'I'm as soun' asleep as a bull-frog,' siz I.

"'Come,' siz she, 'none of yer *nadiums*, but get up and put on the fire.'

"'I think I hear you, ma'am,' siz I.

"'What?' siz she, 'ye lazy, good-for-nothin' scrub ye, do ye mane to say ye're not goin' to do as ye're bid?'

"'Throgs,' siz I, 'there'll be two moons in the sky, an' one in the du'ghill, when ye get me to put on a fire for ye.'

"Faix the word wasn't fairly out of me mouth, when, without sayin' *dhirum* or *dharum*, she ups with her fist an' the next minnit there was more stars dancin' afore me eyes than ivir I seen on a frosty night—she left me as purty a black eye as ye'd maybe ax to look at. Well, I didn't argy the quistion with Nelly, but got up an' put on the fire.

"Nixt mornin' the praties was to be dug for the brakwus.

"'Barney,' siz she, 'throw the spade over your shouldher, an' go out an' dig a basket of tatties.'

"'Why,' siz I, that way—for I was just what ye'd know afeared—'why,' siz I, 'whin me mother was alive long ago (rest her sowl!),' siz I, 'she used to go out an' dig the brakwus for me herself. Seein' that I was always a delicate sort of boy, she allowed the mornin' air didn't agree with me goin' out on the bare stomach.'

"'An' she sayed that?' siz Nelly, raichin'

her han' for the beetle. 'Ye're a delicate boy, throth—except at male times—and we must harden ye a bit,' an' with that she let fly the beetle at me head, as I was makin' for the door; an'—do ye see that mark?" said Barney, exhibiting to me the track of a wound over one eye, which, to my own knowledge, he got in a drunken squabble only a fortnight before.

"Yes," said I, "I see that. But I was of opinion it was Harry Hudy gave you that the night you had the little scrimmage below at Inver."

"Oh, were ye of that opinion, faix?" returned Barney, slightly nonplussed. "There's many an opinion you have—it's a pity they're not worth much. Harry Hudy did give me a blow there, but then it was the ould wound he opened."

"Oh, that explains it," said I.

"Well, Nelly hadn't to ax me the second time to dig the tatties. I went out an' done it as soon as I got meself gathered up again, an' I went afterwards to Dr. M'Clintock an' got thirteen stitches in the split she made in me head. Throth, the doctor could tell ye,

Barney Roddy's Penance 105

ye could ram yer two fists into the hole was in it! Howan'ivir, I seen there was two sides to the quistion, an' that Nelly was detarmined to be master in her own house.

"The very nixt day there was to be a *caman* match between two townlan's, an' I was axed to be one of the players. I tould Nelly so the night afore. She tould her aunts an' the rest of the congregation that they would all go early to see the match. 'But plaise Providence,' siz she to me, 'it's no place for the lake of you, that should be doin' for yer sowl, instead of makin' a tomfool of yerself with a crooked kippeen; an' ye'll lie in yer bed all day the morra!' I was wise enough to keep me tongue in me jaw, an' say nothin'; but in the mornin', sure enough, she packed one of her gran'-aunts away with me breeches, to hide them in a naybour's, and tould me lie in bed all day and say me baids. Hirsilf an' the thribe of divils she had about her, thricked themselves out with ribbands, an' they stharted away for the day's sport, for all the world lake a dhraper's shop goin' out for an airin'. I lay up in bed with no betther amusement than countin' the rafthers above me; an' when I'd have them all counted, I'd sthart them agane in the new, jist to keep me mind occupied; but I'm blissed if I didn't soon get tired of the same amusement, an' I sayed to meself that it was scarcely as good as *caman* playin'; an' I begun to get a trifle restless an' to yawn lake as if I wanted to swally the bed-posts; an' I sayed, come what might, come what may, I would get up an' make meself a dhrop of tay. So I jumped out of bed, an' for want of betther I hauled myself into a red flannel petticoat of Nelly's—och! the sorra take me if I'm tellin' ye a word of a lie— an' but that was the dear petticoat to me. I dhrew on me coat an' waistcoat, an' puttin' on me brogues an' socks, I thought to meself that I could manage to *cuffufle* about through the house rightly for half an hour, in case no one come in. But the red petticoat didn't more nor reach me knees, an' I laughed hearty at meself, the purty figure I cut, but at the same time I was thrimblin' for 'fraid any of the good boys would catch me in the John Heelan'-man kilts; so I detarmined to make for the room if I foun' anyone comin'. An', be the holy poker, it's not long I had to wait till I heard the thramp marchin' up to the dure. In the hoppin' of a sparrow I was in the room, with the dure closed.

"'Barney Roddy? Where are ye, Barney?' was shouted from the kitchen next minnit, an' the heart jumped into me mouth, for I foun' that it was a party of the *caman* players who come to see what was keepin' me. I nivir let on I heard them.

"'It's in his bed asleep the lazy blaguard must be yet, when he should be in his place in the fiel'. Come, to see if we could waken him up,' says one of them. Och! sweet seventy-nine! Here was I in a purty pickle intirely! 'My blessin' on you, Nelly Moriarty, an' if the divil had his own,' siz I to meself, 'it's not showing off yer foldherols an' fineries ye'd be in a *caman* fiel' the day.'

"'Barney Roddy!' agane one of them shouts, givin' the room dure a rattle that I thought I'd have it in a-top of me—'Barney Roddy, are ye there? or what's wrong with ye at all, at all, that ye're not out with yer *caman* an hour ago?'

"I hauls a blanket off the bed, an' rowlin' it about me for feard of the worst, I plants me back to the room dure, an' thinkin' to frighten them away, I shouts back,—

"'Och, there's nothing much wrang with me, barrin' that I'm in bed with a touch of a bed fever I have cotched.'

"'Come now,' siz they, 'none of your skeegwaggin', but open the dure an' get out here to the *caman*, before we burst the ould consarn in on ye.'

"Ah, the sweat begun to come down me face in dhrops the size of a pigeon's egg.

"'Can't yez go away like Christians,' siz I, 'an' let a poor man die in paice.'

"But it was no airthly use. They were detarmined to have me, an' have me they would. So then ivery man put their shouldhers to the dure, an' the next minnit they were in a-top of me. An' there I stood thrimblin' in the middle of the flure, pullin' the blanket closer about me. But as me ill fortune would have it, doesn't one of the lads—there was a whole half-a-dozen of them in it—doesn't one of them eye my brogues peepin' out from undher the blanket!

"'Ah,' siz he, 'here's a go! Does Barney Roddy go to bed in his brogues! Ha, ha! he was thryin' to play us a thrick; but we know one worth two of that.'

"'Ay,' an' siz another blaguard, 'does he usually go to bed with his waistcoat an' coathamore on him?' pullin' open the blanket at the breast.

"'It must be a new midicine for faver patients,' siz another.

"'No, but Barney wants to die an' be berrid in his brogues, sooner nor let any other lucky dog step into his shoes, an' get the widow,' siz another.

"'Ay, an' her twenty-nine aunts,' siz another.

"Then they got a hoult of the blanket to pull it off me, but I held on to it like grim death.

"'Niver mind,' siz the ringleader of the gang, Archy Magee, 'when he's so fond of the blanket we'll laive it with him. Up with him on yer shouldhers, boys, just as he is, an' give him the frog's march to the *caman* fiel'; then let him pride out of the good colour of his blankets there, if he likes—he'll have a repreciative audience.'

"An' before they give me time to open me mouth they had me on their shouldhers, wrapped up like a corp in the blanket, an' away to the *caman* fiel' hot foot. They joulted the sowl out of me so, that purshuant to the one of me could get a word out of me mouth till we got to the fiel', with them hilloain' an' the crowd cheerin', an' all the worl' in commotion to see what they had rowled up in the blanket. Down they planked me with a hearty cheer in the middle of all the spectathors; an' when they pulled the blanket off me by main force, och, holy Moses, but that was the consthernation! It would be hard to tell whether it was them or me or the crowd was the most thundherstruck, to see Barney Roddy come out to play *caman* in a red flannen petticoat that come down to his knees!

"I took to me scrapers, an' the crowd just only then got their tongues loosed, an' they sent up a roar that would make the dead play hop-scotch in their coffins, an' they stharted afther poor Barney, hilloain' an' shoutin' an' laughin'; but, be me boots, I soon distanced them, an' when I got out of their sight I made for the nearest house, scarin' all the childer was in it clane out of the townlan'. I helped meself to the long loan of the best pair of throwsers I could *screenge* up in the house; an' shakin' the dust of that counthry off me feet, I thurned an' bequaithed my left-handed blessin' to Nelly Moriarty an' her breed, seed, and jinnyration, and left for iver a counthry where I could niver more hould up me head to look a man sthraight in the face.

" An' be all that's good there comes that misardly scandaverous villain, Mickey Roarty, an' the neygar 'ill be afther makin' me hop for losin' me day sittin' here spinnin' lies—I mane to say tellin' histhory passages of me life to you. I wish all the crows in Connaught would pick that rascally eye out of his head, an' the dickens fly away with the remaindher of him, for it's him is the blaguard has the bad tongue.—God save ye, Misther Roarty, but this is the purty evenin' intirely, isn't it? "

Dinny Monaghan's Last Keg

Dinny Monaghan's Last Keg

"DINNY MONAGHAN'S, of Keelogs, that's where we're bound for; and Hazelton, my boy, if you only mind your points it's maybe a sergeant you'll be made for this night's work. The ould spite between himself an' Brannigan, you see, is at work still—more power to it—an' we're goin' to reap the fruits. Brannigan come in the whole way to tell me that they brewed last night, an' a mighty big brewin' it was, too—but unknownst to him: but he says they have one of the kegs still in the house, an' they're goin' to have a jorum with some invited naybours to-night; so we'll just give them a bit of a pleasant surprise, an' deil's good cure to Monaghan, he's the biggest rascal ever was born to stretch hemp. The fox runs long, Hazel, my boy—you mind the ould sayin'. Many's the thramp he give us for nothin', but we'll nip his career, the villain, to-night, an' pay him back with compound inthrust. Come, Murphy, Short, Hazelton—are ye all ready? Mount your big coats, for it's an ugly raw night as ivir fell from the heavens. Thramp!"

It was Sergeant M'Golrick, better known as "the Black Sergeant," that addressed his subs. in the Ballynapooka police station, situated among the Donegal hills, upon what the sergeant very aptly described as "an ugly raw night" in March, 185—. And now, as the four cloaked and armed figures disappear from the station in the thick darkness of the night, I will take the story-teller's convenient privilege of whisking my readers direct to Dinny Monaghan's cottage in Keelogs, whence, as we come up to the door, shouts of mirth and hilarity are heard to ring out, as the inmates, all unconscious of the impending danger, are commemorating the successful brewing of the last "run" of mountain dew. As we glide in, and close the door upon the chill, foggy night-air without, a scene meets our view that charmingly contrasts with the rank unpleasantness that

Dinny Monaghan's Last Keg

reigns outdoors. The peat and fir piled high upon the hearth shoot upwards merry, playful, dancing tongues of flame, that send fanciful shadows wavering over the soot-stained rafters aloft, and appear like some blithe, shadowy beings looking down upon the revels below, with restless delight. There is no other light in the cottage, nor is any other needed; the remotest corners of the big kitchen are sufficiently enlightened by the blazing fir, and the merry faces of those who form a wide circle round the big, open hearth are lit up by the red blaze in a picturesque manner. You see that short, black-whiskered man, with the merry twinkle in his eye, who is seated at the upper corner, and is now looking side-wise at the half-filled glass (with the stem broken off) which he holds betwixt his eye and the fire-light—that is no other than the redoubtable Dinny himself, the renowned distiller of forbidden liquors, the "marked man" of innumerable generations of peelers, and the inveterate and unflinching denouncer and renouncer of Excise, Excisemen, magistrates, peelers, and police courts, with all their pomps and vanities. But I daresay you know Dinny and all his characteristics without my description. Who does not? And you must know, too, most all the "old, familiar faces" that circle around—Paddy Teague and Charley the Rooshian, and Billy M'Cahill—a lad who could run a dhrop of the rale stuff as well as the next—Murty Meehan, Mickey *Ruadh*, and the rest of them, not forgetting Mrs. Monaghan—Dinny's plump little wife who is making herself so busy drawing from the "ten-gallon" (that is in the corner above her, just behind an unoccupied cradle), and replenishing the glasses as they are emptied. So we'll just turn our attention to what they are saying.

"Why, Jimmy M'Groarty, did ye get the parrylitics in yer arm, or what's the matther with ye? You same to have forgot the r'yal road to yer mouth; an' throgs if ye have it's a bit change come over yer mother's son. Tip that dhrop over, avic, and don't be makin' mouths at it; ye're nursin' it for the last half-hour like a sick doll that had caught the maisles. Sure ye're not afeard of it? It can't be that it's so ill-tasted; I think I made worse dhrops in my career. Over with it, man, an' give us a song."

"Faix, Dinny, you're right there—here's may we niver dhrink worse!—Hem! Dinny, ye *did* make worse. With due respects I say it. At the same time the worst iver you made would earn a repitition (reputation) for any honest distiller. But it's seldom ye were able to coax anything out of the worm to aiqual that. It's for all the worl' like me fren' there beyant, Paddy Teague's blarney —ha! ha!—it goes down aisy."

"Throth, Jimmy," replies Paddy, "little wondher it goes down aisy with ye—ye're payin' nothin' for it."

This repartee is received with a chorus of laughter.

"By the boots, Paddy, an' it differs from your blarney, then."

"How is that?"

"Why, Paddy Teague nivir blarneyed a man yet—no matther it was his own mother —but that man had to pay through the nose for it."

"Ha! ha! ha! ha!"

"Boys, Jimmy's gettin' witty, wherever

he larned it. It wasn't at school, anyhow; I know that, for ye mind, Jimmy, the masther turnin' ye out be the lug, an' warnin' ye niver to let him see yer purty face again."

"Ha! ha! What was he thurned out for, Paddy?"

"Och, the ould complaint."

"What was that?"

"Why, atin' too much! — I'm sorry, Jimmy, avic, to fetch the flush to yer face, but—"

"Paddy, *ahaisge*, ye don't see any flush on my face."

"Throth, Jimmy, I know we don't see it on yer face, but if it was washed we would. Ye see, boys, it was the time the relief stirabout was givin' out in the bad times, an' Jimmy's father, poor man, sent him to school to gradyate; but Jimmy, the villain, not content with the stirabout, took to atin' the numbers off the noggins.* So the masther give him siveral public riprimands, but it was all no use; he had to turn him out in the rear. Indade, it went again the mas-

* Noggin, a wooden vessel used instead of a bowl.

ther's grain to do it, as he said; an' so long as Jimmy confined himself to *lickin'* the noggins it was of coorse right enough, he said, an' saved the expinses of washin' them; but he had to be responsible to the Gover'ment for the noggins, an' that bein' the case, he said he couldn't permit a cannyball to remain in his school — you'll excuse me, Jimmy, for rememb'rin' this. Keep an eye to Billy M'Cahill there, boys, for I'm afeard he'll go into fits, he's laughin' that hearty at Jimmy."

"No, Paddy asthore, I know what Billy is laughin' at; he's thinkin' of the day your gran'uncle got invested with the hemp collar —the day he danced the double shuffle without a door anondher his feet, ye mind, an' all bekase some of the naybour's sheep took a likin' to go to the fair with his own, and to get sould among them *be mistake*. That's what Billy's laughin' at. He's thinkin', too, how his own gran'father was refused the honour of pullin' the cord an' earnin' a couple of pounds in the mornin'."

"Thrue as gospel, Jimmy," Billy interposes; "but *your* gran'father was too able for mine that mornin'. He offered the shariff to take the job at half-price, an' got it."

"Ha! ha! ha!" laughs Dinny, with the tears actually streaming down his cheeks in thorough enjoyment of the fun he had unconsciously started. "Ha! ha! ha! Jimmy, I'm afeard they'd get too many for ye, ha! ha! ha! Yez 'ill have to give over the *sconsin'** till we have a song. Jimmy, clear yer throat, like a man, an' rattle us up a song."

"Jimmy M'Groarty's song! Jimmy M'Groarty's song!" now resounds from all sides.

"Hould on yez!" interjects Dinny. "Mrs. Monaghan, would ye be so kind as to replinish our empty glasses with a little more goat's milk? We'll relish Jimmy's song the betther of it. That's you, thank ye! Now, boys, here's Jimmy's health, an' long life an' an aisy death to him!"

"An' may I nivir die in the air, ha! ha!" with a significant look at Paddy Teague.

"An' may he nivir pull the rope at half

* Chaffing.

price, though it is in the blood!" retorts Paddy.

This is received with another good-humoured laugh all round, in which Jimmy, of course, takes part. The glasses are emptied with a delightful rapidity, lips are smacked, throats cleared, and Jimmy informs them that he is going to give them "Paddy Shinaghan's Cow."

"Bully for ye, Jimmy!"

Jimmy immediately proceeds to assume the regular orthodox singing attitude. A man attempting to sing without having a voice would scarcely be less unfavourably received than a man singing without the proper attitude. So, in order to acquire this attitude let us attentively observe Jimmy. He first crosses the legs, then insinuates his thumbs into his waistcoat at the armpits, leans well back on his chair, prospects in the roof for a proper rafter at which to pitch his voice—this rafter likewise serves for reflectively swaying the head, and making appropriate gestures at, as well as (apparently) reading the words off—and having found a fitting rafter,

Jimmy commences amid an all but breathless silence:—

"There's a man in Ardaghey both proper an' tall;
Och, he's wan Paddy Shinaghan, we do him call,
For he brews the cordial that does exceed all—
Sure he bates all the docthers aroun' Dinnygal.

"For if ye were gaspin' and ready to die,
The smell of it fastin' would lift yer heart high;
So hoist it up farther, quite near to your nose—
Sure an Inver man loves it wheriver he goes!

"We can't have a christ'nin' without it at all,
We dhrink an' sing chorus, shake hands an' sing all.
Your health now, dear gossip, as I may you call—
Sure if this be's a *ghost*, that it may meet us all!

"Now, Paddy, the rascal—of late it has been—
With steam an' hot wather he brewed his poteen;
He left it in barrels, as I hear them say,
But his cow took a notion of dhrinkin' that day!

"Wirrasthrue! when the cow, sure, the notion did take,
She first broke the *boroch** and then pulled the stake,
Then she dhrunk at the barrels till she dhrunk her fill—
Holy Nelly! she didn't leave much of the still!"

"The sarra take her, but she was fond of the sperrits."

* The rope by which a cow is secured to the stake.

Dinny Monaghan's Last Keg

"Whisht! whisht! *Bedhahosth!* Go on, Jimmy, *ma bouchal!*"

"But when she got dhrunk she began to feel shame,
An' she says, 'Paddy Shinaghan'—call'n' him by name—
'I'm as dhrunk as a beggar, with juice of the malt,
But Paddy, avourneen, it isn't my fault.'

"Then she hiccoughed and staggered an' axed Pat to fight,
An' she threatened that through him she'd let in the daylight;
That his breed was all cowards she tould him to note,
An' dared him to tramp on the tail of her coat.

"Next day she woke up with a bad broken horn,
And begun for to curse the day she was born;
She cursed barley, an' kilty, an' poteen likewise,
An' cursed all the still-tinkers anondher the skies.

"She warned all good cows to mind their fair name,
An' to niver taste dhrink that would fetch them to shame,
An' she whispered to Paddy, an' said in his ear,
'Sure ye will not tell Oonah I went on the beer?

"'An' Paddy, *ahaisge*, if mercy you'll have,
I'll bring ye each year a fine heifer calf,
For I am right honest, though found of a spree,
An' sure, Paddy, *ma bouchal*, ye're as fond of 't as me!'

"An' Paddy had marcy (we give him renown);
But when Oonah did milk her, her milk it was brown.

'Poor cow, then,' says Oonah, 'it's yer heart's
   blood ye give,
For ye won't see us wantin' milk while you do live.'

" Now, we'll dhrink an' be merry, an' forgive the
   cow ;
Here's a health to bould Shinaghan, whither or
   how ;
Let us pray may he never lose head, worm, or still
On that sanctified place they call Keelog's Hill.

" Here's a health to myself, an' God save Ireland's
   King !
Sure it's me makes the valleys of Keelogs to ring,
It's me makes the valleys an' taverns to roar—
Without a dhrop of whisky I can sing no more !"

" Bravo! bravo! Bully, ye are! Hurroo!" is echoed from all quarters.

"Mrs. Monaghan—Biddy—fill his glass, for he deserves it, in throgs. Fill all our glasses when ye're at it, an' we'll dhrink Paddy Shinaghan's health. Here's to him, boys—good fortune."

" Throth, an' it's no mane song," says Charley the Rooshian, up-ending his glass to see that he has drunk it clean.

" Throth no, Charley; nor he was no mane man made it either. It's as purty a rhyme as I came acrass for a considherable time," says Paddy Teague.

Dinny Monaghan's Last Keg

"Thrue for ye, Paddy," adds Jimmy; "he knew how to make rhymes, that man did."

"Oh, he was a shupayrior poet."

"Shupayrior?"

"It's very few of yer 'come all ye's' ye'd get to touch up to it."

"Thry that for a thrick."

"Ay, an' the cow, the poor baste, she acts so nathural like, just for all the worl' like a daicent Christian, axin' Paddy to thramp on the tail of her coat, an' all that, an' then repintin' next mornin'."

"Ay; but," interposed Dinny, "meself wouldn't like to be a barrel of poteen in her way the nixt night again. Ha! ha!"

"Och, jist like the Christian again, Dinny, avourneen."

"Ha! ha! ha!"

"Dinny, *ahaisge*, take you warnin' from that song, an' rair up yer cows in the way daicent cows should be raired. Don't lay timptation, in the shape of a barrel of poteen, in their way. There's a brinley cow ye have, wid no eyes only one, an' that one lookin' crossways with pure divilment, an' I wouldn't thrust but she'd go on the spree in a minnit. She has a rascally bad look about her."

"Nivir fear ye, Mickey, agrah, when I hide me poteen he'll be cleverer than a brinley cow that 'ill fin' it."

"Throth, then, the Black Sargint, they say, has swore that he'll make ye pay the piper yet."

"Well, maybe it wouldn't be the first false oath he swore, if we'd believe all people say. Ha! ha!"

"He's a born divil. There's no being up to his thricks. Dark an' dhirty as the night is, I woudn't at all be very much surprised to see him openin' the door an' marchin' in."

"Is it him? He's measlin' his purty shins at the barrack fire, plottin' some new mischief with the divil. He'd think twicet before he'd come out such a night as that. Biddy, fill us the glasses again; I have one other toast to give before I let yez go, boys—a toast that I'm sure yez'll all do honour to. I'm goin' to toast—thank ye, Biddy!—to toast a man whose kindness or whose mortial great cliverness, or whose love for all poteen-makers, I don't know which yez'll most admire. Now, boys, yez'll have to take off yer glasses cliverly to it—here's 'The Black Sargint.'"

"Here's the Black Sargint!" was shouted—it almost seemed echoed—from the door, which was suddenly burst open, and a breathless youngster leaped into the house.

At the sudden ejaculation from the door, every man present experienced a shock that fetched him instantaneously to his feet, and the mouths that had just opened to laugh at the first mention of the epithet were still held open in consternation at the second unlooked-for, astounding shout of it.

"Here's the Black Sargint!" the lad repeated. "He's on the top of yez. When I seen him an' his men passin' our door, takin' the short cut for here, I got out the back way, an' off to warn ye; but, bad luck to him, he cotched sight of me, an' he didn't let me gain much groun' on him. Holy Moses! that's the thramp comin' roun' the house."

"No way of consailin' the keg!" muttered Dinny, now as pale as a ghost. "Caught at long last, boys!—the jewel are ye, Biddy!—there's a chance for Dinny, yet, boys!

There he is, may the dickens take him, the black rascal! Off, boys, with every dhrop!"

During the utterance of the last few sentences, the door is repeatedly and loudly battered at, and a gruff voice without is angrily demanding admittance. It is no other than the dreaded "Black Sargint." Mrs. Monaghan, you may observe, is, with great coolness, wrapping up and paying much attention to what appears to be a child in the cradle; though hitherto, we feel assured, there did not seem to be any child in it, nor did she pay the slightest attention to the cradle throughout the night. As Dinny proceeds to the door, the men, having emptied their glasses, cast an anxious look in the direction of the keg, but are amazed to see no keg in it. Then, observing Mrs. Monaghan's motions, their faces brighten somewhat.

"Arrah, be aisy would ye at the door, whoiver ye are," says Dinny, as he applies his hand to undo the bolt. "Why, sargint, avic, ye don't mane to say its yerself's in it? Why, I didn't know what sort of a moroder (marauder) was batin' the divil's own tindherary on the door wantin' to pull down an honest man's house. Why, it's yerself's heartily welcome—an' yer fren's, too—one, two, three of them. Gintlemen, this is an unexpected plisure. Now, who'd have thought yez would take it into yer head to come out for a moonlight sthroll sich a night! Mrs. Monaghan, agrah, would ye lave the Rooshian in charge of the wean for a minnit, an' look if ye'd have ever another dhrop in the cubbard for the daicent gintlemen? You haven't a dhrop? *Wirrasthrue*, I'm sorry for that. If yez had had just honoured us by dhroppin' in five minnits sooner, gintlemen, I would have give yez a dhrop would warmed yez down to the exthraymities of yer big toes. *Movrone!* but I'm unlucky!"

"Come, Monaghan, none of yer palaverin'; stan' aside, an' I'll sarch the cubbard, an' a few other places for meself. You've had things purty near long enough yer own way; but Dinny, ould boy, it's my turn now —time about, ye know, is fair play."

"Why, sargint, darlin', sure it's welcome ye are to take a peep into the cubbard, an' pick an' choose for yerself. It's a kindly heart ye have. It's few would lave their warm fire sich a night, and plod four mile, through cowld an' wet, mud and muck, to their fren's. Poor divils! yez are stharved an' drownded, that's what yez are. Push forrid to the fire; don't feel backward. That glass, sargint, jewel, is emp'y, as ye observe. Och, it's no good in ye thryin' any of them —they're all emp'y as yer own skull."

"They are emp'y, I see, but—"

"Och, no 'buts' at all about it, sargint, avic. I'll jus' sen' the youngsther over to Paddy Neddy's, of the back of the hill—he's makin' a runnin' the night (may he have luck with it!), and I'll jist get ye a dhrop of the first shot."

"Come, come, Monaghan," says the sergeant, whose 'dandher' is commencing to rise at Dinny's jokes, "give us no more of your blarney, but tell me where's the poteen you run last night?"

"Where's the poteen I run last night?"

"Yes, where's the poteen you run last night? You have a keg of it in the house—you know you have; an' you'd betther not

Dinny Monaghan's Last Keg

get yer house pulled upside down, but hand it out at oncet, for I'll have it with me, should I pull down yer house to get at it."

"Well, sargint, avic, I daresay the aisiest way is the best, so, if ye promise not to sthir anything else lookin' for more—bekase there's no more in it—I'll tell ye where that dhrop is."

"That's right, Dinny; I see you have some sense afther all. Where is it?"

"Why, sargint, it's—av coorse ye promise what I axed ye?"

"Of coorse, of coorse, man."

"Honour bright."

"Honour bright, Dinny."

"Why thin, sargint, yer a daicent fellow as iver stepped in shoe-leather, so I'll tell ye. It's—*it's in the keg!*"

"The divil take ye! I'll overhaul yer whole house."

"Och, sargint, yer promise! Honour bright, ye know."

"Go to the deuce! When ye won't tell me where the keg is, I'm goin' to find it. Come on, men!"

"Aisy, sargint, aisy, ye didn't ax me where the keg was."

"Stan' aside."

"So you'll pull down a man's house."

"Tell me, then, where is the keg?"

"I will, if you give me that promise."

"I'll give ye the promise; an' more than that, I'll stick to it, if ye tell me *the very place* the keg is."

"The very place—I'll tell ye it."

"All right, then, ye have my promise."

"Well, the keg, sargint—*the very place* the keg is, is *about the poteen!*"

This is greeted by a loud roar from all sides of the house, while Mrs. Monaghan, who has been industriously rocking the cradle all the time, protests,—

"Billy M'Cahill, I would thank ye to not thramp over the wean. Yez have it awake, yez have, with yer jokin' an' laughin'. I'll thurn yez out, ivery mother's sowl, if yez can't have behaviour," and she stoops over the cradle to soothe her charge, whilst the sergeant and his men proceed at once, in mighty wrath, to search for the keg.

"Bad scran to yez, I say again, an' will yez

Dinny Monaghan's Last Keg 135

not fall over the cradle an' smother the chile! Paddy Teague, isn't it near time ye wor thinkin' of goin' home to Norah? I think it's purty near time yez were all thrampin', an' leave a weeny bit of room for the gintlemen to get sarchin' the house," says Mrs. Monaghan.

"Now, Hazelton, try you the room there below, an' meself an' Murphy 'ill thry this other room. Short, throw you your eye about the kitchen here—don't leave a mousehole you won't sarch. Hazelton, my boy, ye were long lookin' for the sthripes—now's yer chance."

"Is it Misther Hazelton get the sthripes?" from one in the crowd, who are now commencing to enjoy the thing. "Throth, he will get them—but, I'm afeard, it 'ill be on the wrong place, ha! ha!"

"Ha! ha! ha! Now, Misther Short, ye boy ye, 'arn you the sthripes."

"Och, be the holy poker, he'll rise in the worl' yet, the same man will."

"How high?"

"Och, meself can't tell that—it all depends on the taste of the hangman."

"Why then, Charley, I dar'say it'll be the *short* dhrop they'll thrate him to, no matther who gets the privilege of pullin' the cord."

"I'm thinkin'—for the Lord's sake, Misther Short, take care of yer prayshus self, ye were a'most down, there—I'm thinkin', boys, it'll be a *very short drop* he'll get to-night, anyhow."

"Throth, then, it'd be a shame to thrate the daicent man so, afther him comin' so far to see yez."

"Ay, an' on such a divil's own wet, dhirty night, too."

"Ay, an' see there's a river of wather runnin' from him, poor man, that would nearly wash a policeman's conscience."

"Ay, if he had it about him. But they say that when they go on duty they have got spayshill ordhers from Dublin Castle to leave their conscience at home behin' them, for fear they would get injured."

"Or maybe lost—I heerd tell of a peeler losin' his conscience when on duty."

"The Lord help the poor man foun' it. I wouldn't like to be in his shoes."

"Why, sargint, avic, is it out of the room

ye are, an' widout the keg? Ye must have been crassed by a red-haired man to-night—ye have no luck."

" Faix, sargint, darlin', it's cowld an' wet an' I dar'say hungry an' thirsty ye are. Pull up to the fire *ahaisge*, an' take a shin-heat."

" The poor man is too fond of his counthry an' it's workin' himself to death he is. Look, he's disappearin' inside his clothes, for all the worl' like a haporth of tibbacky in a sack."

" An' there's poor Hazelton, too, has given up the lower room; an' he's desarvin' of his counthry, if iver a man was—he's shiverin' like a dhrownded cat, an' the teeth in his head's rattlin' like a workhouse cart. Cheer up, oul' fellow, the sthripes is before ye yet."

" Oh, they are *before* him maybe now, but they'll be *behind* him, plaise the Lord, some day."

" Now, Mickey Roe, don't be hard on the poor man; maybe it's enough he's sufferin' this minnit in his own heart, bein' disappointed of the warm dhrop of the crathur he was expectin'."

" In his own *heart!* It's the first time I

iver heerd him accused of havin' one. Where might he carry the article?"

"In his stomach."

"Or in his heels? It was in his heels he had it the day that Peggy M'Glanaghan ducked him in the du'ghill pit, an' then chased him for his life."

Whilst this running commentary was kept up amid peals of laughter by the crowd around the fire, the poor peelers were ransacking and rummaging the house in all directions, and receiving the chaff with a very bad grace indeed; which fact, of course, made it still the more enjoyable to the jesters, and held out the stronger incentive for them to pepper the four unfortunate poor fellows still more unmercifully. Mrs. Monaghan, all the time, was industriously attending to the slumbers of "the crathur" in the cradle, hushing its restless *spirit* to repose, and crooning a lullaby to aid the good object. Occasionally, too, she would stoop down, say a few soothing words, bestow a kiss apparently on its little brow, and cover it up snugly. This she would sometimes vary, by addressing a pettish remonstrance to the men to keep their tongues at rest, and not disturb "the crathur's" slumbers. She sat between the cradle and the fire, with her deep shadow cast upon it. The police are now getting thoroughly tired of their search, the evidence of their own eyes, coupled with the coolness and fearless tone of Dinny and his party, inducing them to believe that there cannot possibly be a keg in the house —whatever little they had within, they must have just finished as they (the invaders) entered. Of course they could not sustain a prosecution upon the strength of the smell (or the smell of the strength) of the glasses. They are about to depart, but Hazelton— the stripes still floating in his mind's eye— must search the top of the dresser. For this purpose, he leans upon the shoulder of the sergeant, and stepping on the rim of a tub of dirty water which had been used for washing roots in, he succeeds in satisfying himself that there is no contraband material on it, when, unluckily, his weight on the one side of the tub upsets it, and tumbles him flat just in time to receive its contents. In the act of falling he has fetched down his worthy sergeant beneath him, who acts as a buffer between Hazelton and the floor, and comes in for half the contents of the tub. A shout of laughter that seems almost to shake the old roof greets this ludicrous *dénouement,* and the sergeant and Hazelton get up, glare at each other for a moment, shake themselves like spaniels, and then take their solemn departure in rather a crestfallen manner, and are slowly followed by their two companions with arms unconsciously reversed, all followed by the jeers and hilarious merriment of the inmates. We will not undertake to describe the scene that followed inside—the praises loudly lavished on Mrs. Monaghan, the fondling "the crathur" got, the mutual congratulations and exultations, the drinking of Mrs. Monaghan's health, the drinking of Dinny's health, the drinking of the company's health, the drinking of everybody's health—not neglecting the Black Sergeant's—and the drinking of the *doch an dorrish,* and the final dispersion of the company, which ended the eventful night. It was a night to be remembered.

Billy Baxter

Billy Baxter

Now, Billy wasn't a religious man. That's certain. He was, I fear, a wicked, worldly-minded sinner; too frequently the cause of distress and of much spiritual anxiety to the righteous among his Cruckagar neighbours. He had a sinful habit of weighing all actions, even the most edifying religious ones, in a worldly scale of his own that was the cause of much scandal and many heart-burnings to those good ones around him whose thoughts ran upon the world which has its hither boundary in the silent churchyard. Within the memory of our dogmatic Oldest Inhabitant, Billy had only been twice to his church—one of which occasions was at his marriage to Jane. Whenever the O. I. had occasion to bear sorrowful testimony to Billy's laxity, he invariably shook his head, and, in half an hour after, there were not three heads unshaken in all Cruckagar for "Billy Baxther, the Lord forgive him!—no better nor the black haithen!" When remonstrated with on the point Billy was unconsciously — quite innocently — satirical: "Sure where anondher the sun is the good of me goin' to prayer or meetin', that never, since I was no bigger nor me knee, was masther of a shoot of clothes that me naybour 'ud turn on his heel to look at?" Billy, in short, looked upon church as a luxury and a frivolity intended for the idle and the vain, and altogether out of the sphere of a hardworking poor man, who, willy nilly, must take life seriously. "By right," as we put it, Billy should be a Presbyterian; which is to say that his parents were understood to have belonged to that Church.

The Rev. Ezekiel M'Cart was the Presbyterian pastor of Cruckagar. He was a typical minister of the Gospel—pious as a saint, learned as a doctor, simple as a babe, humble, and, withal, poor as the poorest of his small and miserably poor congregation. Mr. M'Cart, notwithstanding an innate esthetic dread of his free-thinking parishioner, considered that it would be a shirking of his duty if he didn't remonstrate with Billy. He did so, asking him to quit the ways of the unrighteous and come back to his church and his spiritual duties. For Mr. M'Cart alone, of all the clergymen he knew, Billy had a huge esteem—the humility and simple-mindedness and unobtrusive goodness of the man had secretly won him. So, with profoundest respect, he lent a most attentive ear to the good man's exhortations, and when he had finished, Billy said:

"Now, yer reverence, out of regards to ye, I'll put me foot in the fire if ye bid me do it, but I'll not go to Meetin'. I have been there afore, expectin' to hear somethin' might do me good—for God knows I'm in black need of 'mendment!—but I heerd nothin' only scouldin' the divil. I heerd Misther Mahon praich wanst, an' he did nothin' only scould the divil. I listened for two hours to the Methodist praicher, an' it was bally-raggin' the divil from commencement to end. Twicet I went to hear Father Dan, an' it was pitchin' in to the poor divil with him, too, as hot as he could pepper him. That gave me my fill of church, chapel, an' meetin'. The divil may be bad—an' I'm not denyin' but he is—but the poor fellow's not gettin' half a chance. An' if he's as bad as yez make him out, small blame to him, say I, for if he had the spirit of a dog, he couldn't take off yer hands all yez give him from June to January, an' be otherwise nor bad, an' the worst of bad."

After that conversation, the good Mr. M'Cart, shocked beyond expression, let Billy go his way in peace, for he saw well that counsel was lost on him.

I said Mr. M'Cart was poor. Father Dan was the lucky owner of a jaunting car and a mare, Forgiveness, both of which, if neither dashing nor handsome, were useful. Mr. Mahon, the rector, richly dressed, invariably drove an extremely smart turn-out. Even the Methodist preacher had to confess to a conveyance of a certain primitive and homely character. Mr. M'Cart alone had to trot the length and breadth of a tedious parish on Shanks' mare, which is to say, his own two feet, with the added luxury of a stout stick. This was not as it should be. His little flock, who loved the man dearly, saw this, and said it shouldn't be. Nixon Beattie and Andy Ritchie were appointed to take their mites from their poor brethren that their pastor might be lifted out of the mud, and on horseback hold up his head with his fellows. Should they, the collectors asked themselves, call upon the black sheep? They would—though in all probability they'd get small thanks and less money. But grievously they mistook their man. Billy was overjoyed at being enabled to contribute towards the well-being and the ease of him whom he so much admired. From his hoard in the old stocking in the chimney—a hoard of silver and coppers amounting probably to not less than five and twenty shillings—he drew forth a shining white shilling, and ringing it on the table to them, wished from his soul that it had been a sovereign, "For," Billy said, "we must try to buy him somethin' worthy of him, an' a credit to us." He already felt the pride of part ownership.

Ten days later a deputation, each member of which was, in solemn conclave, elected on the strength of his knowledge of horseflesh, proceeded to the great horse fair of The Moy, and therefrom led back, and proudly presented to their worthy pastor, a comely and very spirited young pony. The good man's sincere protestations that he wished not to accept their too handsome present—that he had not the slightest experience of riding horseback, and that anyhow he thought he should feel ever so much more at home among them travelling to their doors with only his stick—were all of no avail. He was compelled to accept the gift, by none more warmly, more noisily, or more prominently than by Billy Baxter, who, in his folded shirt sleeves—for he had left his spade standing in the ridge—arrived at the Manse just as Adam Lindsay, who kept a grocery, and had oratorical ambitions, was opening up the subject in a very rhetorical, carefully prepared speech. For a few minutes Billy had listened to Adam in a puzzled fashion; he then asked a neighbour, rather audibly, "What the divil is Adam bletherin' about?" and without waiting for answer, stepped in front of the orator and apologetically said:

"Adam, yer reverence, manes to say that we've put our heads together an' bought a bit of a baste for ye, an' there he is "—here Billy gave the pony a smart slap that caused the beast to rear and prance to the imminent danger of the frightened assembly—" an' may the Lord give ye good of him! That's all."

Whilst the self-denying poor man was protesting, the pony was led away and safely stabled. Billy hadn't got time to view the animal to his content and put his merits to the test. He was impatient to satisfy himself. Ten days later, as he dug in his potato field, he saw on the road, which was a few fields distant, his minister ride by upon the new pony; for Mr. M'Cart had with much trouble, mental and physical, mastered the feat of keeping a fairly good seat in the saddle as the pony jogged.

"Hi! hi!" Billy hailed, motioning with his finger that he wished the minister to await him.

He drew rein, wondering what Billy wanted with him. As Billy neared, he found his eye was upon the beast scrutinisingly, not on himself. When Billy came on the road he folded his arms and surveyed the animal's points with the eye of a connoisseur, his head poised on one side. He walked all round the horse so, at a distance of a few yards, breathing a subdued half whistle as he did so. He came forward and lifted one of the fore feet, saying sternly, "Hold up, sir! Hold—up—sirrr!" and having satisfied himself that there wasn't a stone in it, laid it down, and retrograded till he had the animal at the proper angle of observation again.

"Go ahead!" he said abruptly.

Mr. M'Cart said, "Good day, Billy!" and, not without some wonder, went ahead.

"That'll do!" Billy said as abruptly, when the pony had progressed about twenty yards.

Still puzzled, the reverend rider obeyed Billy's terse behest, and stopped short.

"Head him round an' come back. Off you!—off you! There—don't jibe him!—don't jibe him!—for the sake of the Lord don't jibe the baste, yer reverence! Walk him quicker. That's you. Very good—very good, by the powdhers," he remarked to himself.

Taking him by the head when the pony came up, he asked—

"How does he lead?"

But without waiting for an answer he had started off, hauling the pony to a canter, which caused the inexperienced rider to hump himself for safety and tightly press his knees against the beast's sides. He was jolted and thrown about, sometimes on the saddle, but oftener off it, altogether, alas! forming a cruelly undignified picture. Several times he essayed to request Billy to stop, but the words were snapped in his mouth; besides, he almost bit off his tongue in the attempt. Billy, observing his fright, tried to encourage him. As he ran he spoke over his shoulder in a sympathetic voice. He said:

"Dammit, yer reverence, don't be narvous. Don't be narvous, man alive. Grip like the divil, an' houl' on like grim death. That's you," he said, as Mr. M'Cart just narrowly escaped coming down where the horse was not, "ye'll soon be a thunderin' fine rider —a bully rider."

Then when Billy had trotted the horse far enough in that direction to satisfy himself, he drew up, to the great relief of the breathless and frightened equestrian. Billy turned the pony's head, with the intention of experimenting back again to their starting point. But the pony evidently had a will of his own, and he now chose to show it. Instead of starting back with Billy, he threw up his head and pulled in the other direction.

"Oh, ye would, would ye? ye divil ye!" Billy said, as he gave him a sounding whack on the ribs, the good minister's left leg coming in for share of it.

When the pony had thrown up his head and sprung backwards, Mr. M'Cart found himself seated on the animal's neck, very nearly; and when, in acknowledgment of Billy's little remonstrance on his ribs, he sprang forward, the worthy man found himself sitting in uncomfortable proximity to the beast's tail. The third spring brought the saddle under him; the horse had come to a dead pause, and for the first time Mr. M'Cart was enabled to speak.

"William, William, my dear friend," he appealed, "do leave the animal to himself and he'll go like a lamb."

"Ho-o-o! Misther M'Cart," Billy said, "ye're early beginnin' to spoil the baste. 'Spare the rod,' ye know. No, no," and Billy gave the beast another vigorous blow on the ribs; "no, no, we must taich him breedin' or atween us we'll make a purty baste of him." Another whack and another spring, and Mr. M'Cart enclasped the animal's neck in a firm embrace. "No, no, we must taich him who's masther, an' who's man, we must. Houl' on, ye sowl ye—houl' on, Misther M'Cart; I'll soon"—(whack! whack!)—"take the tanthrums out of him!"

"William! William! I do appeal to you——"

"Damn it, yer reverence, ye have no grit in ye. Aisy, ye divil ye! Ha-a-a, take that! Lord, man, ye're as 'feered as fire!"

"William, let me dismount, I beseech you!"

"Och, the divil a wan o' ye is goin' to dismount the day, to plaise him. Take that, ye conthrairy schoundril ye! I'm sure, that's what would spoil him out an' out. Take yer time till—(whack! whack!)—till I'm finished with him. I houl' ye for the biggest button on yer frock, he hasn't as many—(whack! whack!)—as many 'nadiums' in his head when I'm done."

The animal was now prancing around and around in a circle, Billy coolly holding on, endeavouring to magnetise the animal by his eye, but assisting the action with a plentiful shower of blows, most of which fell on the horse, but an occasional one upon Mr. M'Cart, in which case Billy always begged pardon. The hat had fallen forward over the good man's eyes, and as he could not on peril of his life spare a hand to adjust it, he was struggling in the dark.

"Ha-a-a! ye brute ye! Ha-a-a! Take that, ye baste! Ye have the 'stiadh'* in ye, but I'll take it out of ye, or my name isn't Billy. Houl' on, Misther M'Cart, an' don't be freckened—ye're as safe as if ye were in yer arm-chair."

It might be so, still at that instant Mr. M'Cart would have preferred the arm-chair.

* The spirit of contrariness.

Billy Baxter

At length Billy got the "nadiums" out of the animal. He quieted down and went along slowly and quietly with his victor, who experienced not a little silent pride. Though he still continued looking up at the animal and saying "Ha-a-a!" through his teeth to him, more surely to fasten the spell upon him. When he had got him to the point from which he had started, Billy let him go, and said:

"Now, Mr. M'Cart, ye have ten poun' a betther horse nor ye had twinty minutes ago. Ye want to be firm—ye want to be firm. Throth I'm sore afeerd yer reverence would 'a' spoilt the baste in less nor no time—spoilt him! We'd never get no good o' him if ye'd let him do his own biddin.' It was a sthruggle to get the animal, yer reverence, an' now we have him, we must take all the care of him we can. I thrust yer reverence sees he gets a warm mash every night; put a thrifle o' bran through his corn, too— don't forget that; an' see he's properly rubbed down, now, every time he comes in off a journey. Throth, Misther M'Cart, I'm afeerd ye have too many other matthers in yer head; an atween thinkin' of sinners an' sarmons, ye'll let our little baste go to the deuce. That'll not do—that'll never do at all, at all. I'll be keepin' my eye out, now, back an' forrid, to see that he's properly looked afther. Good mornin'—good mornin', yer reverence, an' good luck! An' don't neglect our little animal, mind, whatsomiver ye do!"

Then Mr. M'Cart rode forward in perplexed meditation, whilst Billy crossed the fields again to resume his work, often pausing to cast an anxious glance after the animal, and thereupon invariably shaking his head, as doubtful of the care which should be bestowed upon his property when he wasn't there to see and direct.

Mrs. M'Partlan was an extremely rich old widow lady from Belfast, a pious Presbyterian who had come down to Donegal with the intention of finding out the state of her poorer co-religionists there. Mr. M'Cart had somewhere managed to borrow a phaeton into which he received her off the mail coach at Donegal. At first the pony had showed too much mettle to suit her nerves, but he soon quieted down, so that they got along

Billy Baxter 157

smoothly, till at length, nearing their destination, Mr. M'Cart was not a little unnerved seeing Billy Baxter at work in the same field from which he had before sallied down upon him. But there was a chance of getting past unnoticed. He prayed in his heart that he might. Mrs. M'Partlan, besides being nervous, was cold and hungry, and was (under these conditions) more or less irritable. Billy did not seem to notice their approach. They had already got opposite to him—past him, and the good man was warmly congratulating himself on the narrow escape: but—

"Hi! Hi! Hi! there, I say!"

There was no use pretending not to hear him. Billy was bounding over ditches in his eagerness to catch up to them, and, being fleet of foot, he could accomplish this without difficulty.

"Good morra, yer reverence! Ye're welcome, good woman! Why, ye were near past anonst* to me," Billy said breathlessly as he got up, and with the sleeve of his vest began rubbing off a few flecks of froth that lay on

* Unknown.

the animal's side. "Ye didn't see me? I was levellin' broo's in the fiel' beyant. How is the powny doin', yer reverence? Did ye do as I was— Dammit! man, what manes this?" and Billy proceeded to unhook a curb from the bit. "Tare-an'-ouns! man, don't do that—don't desthroy the little animal's mouth. Or what the divil put it in yer head anyhow. There ye are," and Billy tossed the curb into the phaeton. "Now, that's the height o' nonsense, yer reverence, an' can only give our baste a bad name." Here he got down on one knee in front of the horse and narrowly examined his forefeet. "Upon me sowl," he said, "I do believe he forges. If he does, we're taken in. Just start him along a bit at an aisy canther till I see for meself, an'—"

"But, William, my dear friend, this is a lady friend, Mrs. M'Partlan, and——"

"Yis, yis; sure I spoke to her," Billy said, raising his caubeen, however, to acknowledge the introduction. "How are ye, Mrs. M'Partlan? I suppose you've come over to see Irelan'? Ye'll see plenty o' hardships and hard work. This is the back o' Godspeed, ma'am. I'm plaised for the honour of meetin' ye, ma'am.—Now, yer reverence, ye sowl ye," he continued in the tone of one who had dutifully acquitted himself of a task, "throt him out till I obsarve his steps."

Mr. M'Cart resignedly did as he was ordered.

When he had gone a hundred yards—

"That'll do—that'll do," Billy said. "He just forges the slightest little taste imaginable. But with care we'll br'ak him off it —with care. Ye'll have to give him more of his head, yer reverence—ye'll have to give him more of his head. If ye keep continually naggin' an' naggin', ye'll dhrive the baste to the deuce. Lord, man, give him rein—give him rein, and don't be afeerd. Let him go like blazes if he wants to. Now, there's a great dale in turnin' a baste round. I should like to see how yer reverence manages in turnin' him. Just take him round there, an' drive him back a score o' steps, an' turn him again "—

"But, William, my friend Mrs. M'Partlan——"

"Yis, yis," William said hastily; "ye made the good woman known to me afore. I was spaikin' to Mrs. M'Partlan——"

"She feels it so awfully cold——"

"Yis, ma'am, that's Irelan' for ye. The day we have it as cowl' as charity. Less nor a month ago it was as hot as the hob of the Bad-place, ma'am. Now, Misther M'Cart——"

"She feels both cold, William, and hungry, and would like to get to the manse with as little delay as possible. So, my good friend, if you would——"

"Oh! oh! Surely! surely! Why didn't ye say that afore? Oh, to be sure, me good woman—to be sure! I'll be sayin' good day to ye, Mrs. M'Partlan, an' take good care o' yerself; but ye're in good hands, throth, when ye're in Misther M'Cart's. Ye'll never know how to be half thankful to him. Good day to ye, ma'am. An' good day, Misther M'Cart. Whip him up now, an' off like blazes, both of ye. Good day, good day!"

Mr. M'Cart went off sorely vexed for his peevish companion, who was in high ill humour over the amazing scene.

She was very soon to see their friend again, however. Next day in the little dining-room of the humble manse there sat down to dinner with Mr. M'Cart, Mrs. M'Partlan and her favourite clergyman from Belfast, who was then in the neighbourhood (a solemn dignitary), and a Presbyterian Doctor of Divinity from an adjoining parish. After dinner had begun there was a knock at the door, and without awaiting a response the door was shoved open, and, hat in hand, bowing familiarly to the company, Billy Baxter walked in. Billy was not dressed for dinner either; he wore a sleeved waistcoat, and there was more hayseed and other such material upon his soft hat than etiquette countenances in polite company. But he was nothing abashed.

"Oh, don't—don't, gentlemen, disturb yerselves at all, at all—fire away! an' more power to yer elbows. I only just dhropped in, Misther—How do you do, oul' woman? Excuse me for not seein' ye. But there's such a sight of quality present, I didn't notice ye"—

Here Billy drew himself a chair, and seating himself on it, he reached his hat to the table and placed it there, not far from the plate of the startled Mrs. M'Partlan.

"I hope, ma'am, ye have the appetite good? There's nothing like the appetite. I have a roarin' one. I can ate like a horse, I'll tell ye——"

"William," said Mr. M'Cart, endeavouring to be as conciliating as possible, whilst he removed the offending hat and placed it elsewhere. "William, you wanted to see me?"

"Oh, just, yer riverence, I have only half a word to say to ye. It's about our little powny. I wasn't—Is that what ye call wine now, that the oul' woman's dhrinkin'? It's a dhirty wash, ma'am, no better nor ditch-water, an' tarnation bad for the stomach. There's nothin' better to yer vittils nor a dhrop of prime whiskey. But, sure, I needn't tell you—ye didn't live in the same town of Belfast for a centhury without knowin' that. Misther M'Cart never tastes it himself, ma'am, so ye must excuse him for not havin' it on the table. I'll tell ye, ma'am, where——"

"William, will you come with me, till——"

"Oh, no, no, no, Misther M'Cart! Not at all! Just keep yer sate, I only want half a word, an' I'll be gone."

"Perhaps you'll have some wine, William?"

"No, yer reverence, none of yer slob-wash for me—no disparagement to yer reverence. But, as I was sayin', havin' nothing much else to do this evenin', I dhropped over to have a peep at the powny. I stepped into the stable, an' bad luck to the wan o' me but was up to my knees in it. Yer reverence should send that boy o' yours packin' —he has yon stable in a odious state—there's a 'ho-go' in it would knock ye down. I haven't got it out of my nose yet. Ram it, yer reverence, it'll never do. Aither that divil's kid of a boy ye've got 'ill be dismissed, or else you an' I'll fall out. Then that powny's not gettin' his mait—I do believe that. There wasn't as much hay as ye'd wipe her nose with in the hay-rack, an' that scoundhrill of a lad o' yours down pitchin' buttons with all the blaguards of the counthry at the Cross Roads, when he should be attendin' to the baste, an' givin' him somethin' to keep him from starvin'. An', moreover—Lord, ma'am, is there a bone in yer throat? Clap her on the back, Misther M'Cart!"

But the contortions of Mrs. M'Partlan's face were only the result of indignant amazement.

"An' besides, Misther M'Cart, I don't b'leeve that little blaguard is mixin' bran with the baste's corn as I allowed. Ye should see to it yerself, man, that the little powny gets a warm mash every night. Ye should make it yer business to go down to the kitchen an'—Misther M'Cart, don't forget yer company; here's a gintleman, an' his plate wants renewin', I think—go down, I say, to the kitchen yerself, and see that the pratie skins an' the other scran from the dinner is mixed with it, an' rumble yer han' about through it, too, to see that there's no fish bones, nor the like, in it; an' to see that it's the proper hait. Aisy, good man, or ye'll flow over that tumbler an' spoil the tablecloth, an' that'll fetch Shusan about yer lugs

—faith, don't fetch Shusan down on ye, or she'll let ye know how many bains make five. That's all I've got to say, yer reverence. Only, ye'd betther see that the off-hind shoe is fastened or ye'll lose it. Send the young fellow over to the forge early in the mornin' to have it fastened, or if ye let him go another day he'll lose it, an' ye'll fetch the powny home limpin' like a cripple. An' don't forget to give that youngsther his walkin' papers, an' let him go to the divil to look for a masther. Good day to yez, gintlemen, an' much good may it do yez! Good day to yerself, oul' woman! Ye can send Shusan—give her fourteen pence, an' send her, an' she knows where to go, an' she'll fetch ye as good a dhrop of the rale stuff, I'll stake me voracity, as ye were accustomed to in Belfast. Good day, ma'am; good day! Good day to yerself, Misther M'Cart! an' I hope I didn't put ye about. Don't forget the mash! Rumble yer hand through it yerself, for fear of bones. Send the young blaguard packin' to the divil about his business. Oh, don't be annoyed, ma'am, that's only hayseeds is fallin' off me oul' hat—an' that's a sthraw—let me take that sthraw out o' yer wine. There ye are! Good day all! Good day! I'll call roun' soon again till we have a chat about the baste, yer reverence. Good day, an' good luck!"

But Mr. M'Cart feared too much another interview with Billy. The poorer Presbyterians in the parish of Cruckagar sowed their land that spring with seed purchased by the sale price of the Subscription Horse, whilst with renewed vigour and cheerfulness Mr. M'Cart again trudged his parish on foot, more than ever the idol of good-hearted Billy Baxter.

The Counsellor

The Counsellor

I WOULD not venture to say decidedly whether the Bummadier or Owen a-Slaivin was the better story-teller. I feel quite incapable of pronouncing a definite opinion. Of course we had our men who laughed to scorn the idea of Owen daring to aspire to comparison at all; whilst, likewise, we had those who swore by Owen. Of course, the Bummadier, for the benefit of his worshippers, had placed on record his fixed conviction that a lie never choked Owen; but, as a set-off against this, I may mention that Owen had confidently stated to his intimates there was not a bigger liar nor the Bummadier from * * * (a certain locality I hesitate to mention) to Guinealand. I suppose, however, that in story-telling mere truth is only a matter of detail.

The style of the Bummadier's narratives

was bright, brisk, and lively, and the pleasing shades they presented somehow withheld you from examining too closely into their texture.

In Owen's cabin you would need to sit some time before you discovered the features of your fellow-rakers: the cabin was low, and small, and smoky: his fire, without fir, aimed only at warmth—hence a good part of the indistinctness which clothed the details of the interior. Taking its tinge from the surroundings, then, Owen's style was sombre; and the more comical the story, the more solemn was his manner. An eavesdropper who knew not the man, hearing only the droning tone of Owen, and seeing (through the keyhole) the dim cluster of faces in the dark room, might easily conclude that a flesh-creeping ghost story was in progress— but he wouldn't eavesdrop for long until he would be surprised out of his conclusion.

We would, on the wildest night in winter, travel far and fare ill to hear a story of Dan —the Great Dan—from the most indifferent shanachy. But, to hear it from the lips of Owen—!

The Counsellor

Och, the likes of Dan—the heavens be his bed!—never was known afore, nor will his likes ever be seen again as long as there's a bill on a crow. He was the long-headedest man—glory be to God!—ever stepped in shoe-leather.

There was wanst and there was a poor boy up for murdher—he fell foul of a friend in a scrimmage, and he cracked his brain-box for him without intendin' it, an' the poor man died. An' the short an' the long of it was this poor boy was taken up for the murdher of his frien' with no chance whatsomiver for escape, bekase the evijence was straight an' square that it was him, an' none other, give him the dyin' blow. An' that maint hangin', the poor boy knew well; for in them days they'd sthring ye up for a dickens sight smaller matther.

Well, lo and behould ye! it was the mornin' of the thrial, an' the poor boy, Heaven knows, was down-hearted enough, an' his friends all cryin' round him, thryin' to get him to keep up his spirits, though they knew, too, that it was a hopeless case. All at wanst, it sthruck one of his friends, an' says he,—

"It's a bad case, no doubt, but what harm to consult Counsellor O'Connell?"

Faith, the poor boy leaped at it.

"Consult the Counsellor," says he, "for the Lord's sake! It's small's the chance; but still-and-all, if there's a ghost of a chance he'll see it."

No sooner sayed than done. They had Dan on the spot in three hops of a sparrow, an' explainin' the whole case to him. When Dan heered the outs and ins of it, he shook his head.

"It's a purty straight case," says Dan.

"Is there no chance at all, at all, Counsellor?" says they.

"The Queen's son," says he, "couldn't be saved on the evijence. In spite of all the Counsellors in the counthry, an' if ye had Sent Patrick himself to plead for ye, ye'd be sentenced," says he.

This was the last blow for the poor pres'ner, an' ill he took it.

But all of a suddint, Dan looks him purty hard in the face—

"If I don't mistake me much," says Dan, says he, "ye're a purty bould, fearsomless fella?"

The Counsellor 173

"Och," says the poor fella, says he, "the day was an' I was all that, but I'm thinkin' that day 'ill never come again."

"Well," says Dan, says he, "I have considhered the whole question over, an' if ye're a right boul' fella, and act right boul', out of nine hundher and ninety-nine chances you have just wan half chance for yer life."

"What is it?" says the poor fella, jumpin' at it.

"It's this I'm goin' to tell ye," says Dan. "When your case is heerd, the jury without lavin' the box 'ill return a vardict of 'Guilty, me Lord!' an' his Lordship 'ill then mount the black cap for the purpose of condemnin' ye. You're at that instant to have all the wee narve ye can about ye, an' havin' yer brogue loose upon yer foot, ye're to stoop down an' get a good grip of it in yer fist, an' the minnit ye see his Lordship open his mouth to sentence ye, take good sudden aim, an' with all the veins of yer heart give him the brogue fair atween the two eyes—then laive the rest to Providence."

Thrue enough, it was a quare advice, an' maybe the poor lad didn't think so—but then it was Dan O'Connell's advice, an' that put another face on matthers. When Dan sayed it, it was worth thryin'; so he observed it to the letther; an' when the jury was bringin' in their verdict of "Guilty, me Lord!" he was gettin' his brogue loose on his foot; an' when the Judge got on the black cap, he got a good grip of the brogue, and gathered all his narves, an' the very next minnit, as the Judge opened his mouth to give him sentence, he ups with the brogue, an' with all the powers of his arm an' the veins of his heart, let him have the full weight of the brogue fair atween the two eyes, an' knocks him over flat. An' *a stor! a stor!* up was the Judge agin in an instant, an' him purple in the face, an' he guldhers out,—

"My vardict is that the scoundhril be burned, beheaded, and hung!"

"Aisy, aisy, I beg yer pardon, me Lord," says Dan O'Connell, jumpin' up in his place in the coort. "I beg yer Lordship's pardon," says he, "but I think ye have thransgressed yer rights," and he handed up to the Judge the book of the law that he might see for himself. "Ye can't," says he, "ac-

The Counsellor

cordin' to English law as prented in that book in black and white, sentence a man to be both burned, beheaded, an' hung. Pres'ner," says Dan, then says he, turning to the dock, "pres'ner, you're at liberty to go free." An' the sorra his mouth could the dumbfounded Judge open, as the pres'ner stepped out of the dock a free man, for he saw Dan had him squarely.

Well, there was again, an' there was a poor man, who had got some ha'pence, an' he speculated on a dhrove of cattle, an' started up to Dublin with them to sell them, an' make profit on them. As me brave man was dhrivin' the cattle down Dublin sthreet, out comes a man that kep' a tibbacky shop, a cliver lad, an' he saw his chance, an' sez he to the man who owned the cattle,—

"How much," sez he, "will ye take for the best an' worst of them cattle of yours?"

Well, the poor man looked at the best baste in the dhrove, an' at the worst baste, an' he prices the two o' them in his own mind, an'—

"I'll take so-much," sez he, mentionin' it.

"All right," sez the other, "I'll give ye

yer axin'." An' into his yard he had the whole dhrove dhriven. It was no use whatsomiver for the poor man to object, for the other said he bought the best an' the worst of the cattle, which was all of the cattle, an' he had witnesses to prove it.

Away the poor man, in spite of himself, had to go with the price of barely two bastes in his pocket in payment for his whole dhrove, an' away he went lamentin', an' not knowing how he'd face back to his family again, with their wee trifle of money as good as gone. That night he put up in a public-house, an' the woman of the house comin' to larn the poor fella's lament axed him why he didn't go to the Counsellor, an' have his advice on it. If it did him no good, she said, it couldn't anyhow do him no harm, an' if there was wan way in a thousand out of it Dan would soon find that way.

Right enough, the very next mornin' to the Counsellor the poor man set out, an' laid a full programme of his case afore Dan, an' axed him could anything be done. No answer Dan give him, till first he took three turns up an' down the parlour; and then,—

The Counsellor

"Yis," sez Dan, "somethin' can be done. There's wan way you can get back yer cattle, an' only wan."

"What's that?" sez the man.

"You'll," sez Dan, sez he, "have to cut off the small toe off yer left foot, an' go an' bury it on Spek Island,* an' when you've done that come back to me."

As he was diracted he done with no loss of time, an' back to Dan he comes for further diractions.

"Now," sez Dan, "come along with me."

An' off both of them started an' never halted till they were in the tibbackinist's shop. An' och, it was welcome Dan was with the lad behind the counther, who was bowin' an' scrapin' to him, an' thankin' him for the honour he done him comin' into his shop.

"Can ye sarve me," sez Dan, sez he, "with a little piece of good tibbacky?"

"I can," sez the lad, "sarve yer honour with as good tibbacky as ever ye put intil a pipe-head."

"An' have ye much of it?" sez Dan.

* Spike Island, in Cork Harbour.

"More nor you'd care to buy," sez the lad.

"Now what," sez Dan, sez he, "would ye be afther chargin' me for a sizable piece—say as much as would reach from me fren's nose to the small toe of his left foot?"

The lad laughed at the quality of the ordher, but he knew Dan's odd ways. So, he sized the man up and sez he,—

"I'll take so much," mentionin' some few shillin's.

"It's a bargain," sez Dan.

But lo an' behould ye! when the lad went to misure it he finds the toe gone.

"There's no toe here!" sez he.

"I know there isn't," sez Dan. "Me frend buried it in Spek Island a few days back. Ye'll have to carry on the tibbacky till ye git there."

The lad laughed heartily at this, as bein' wan of Dan's best jokes.

But Dan didn't laugh at all, at all.

But, "Troth, an'," sez he, "I hope ye'll be laughin' when ye've finished misurin' me out me bargain."

"Och, Counsellor, yer honour," sez the

lad, sez he, "but sure ye don't railly mane it? Isn't it jokin' ye are."

"I tell ye what it is, me good man," sez Dan back to him, "you misure me out me bargain, an' be very quick about it, too; or, if ye don't," sez he, "be all the books in Chrissendom, I won't laive a slate on yer roof, or a stick or stave on yer primises I won't sell out till I have paid meself the sum of five thousan' poun' for braich of conthract," sez he, "an' here's me witness."

"It's ruinated I am entirely, out an' out," sez the lad.

"It's ruinated ye desarve to be," sez Dan. "Ye thought little of ruinatin' this poor sthranger here beside me, when he come up to Dublin with his little grain of cattle, sthrivin' to make a support for the wife an' childre. It's ruinated ye ought to be, ye lowlifed hang-dog ye! Turn the daicent man out his cattle this instant, in as good condition as you got them, an' moreover nor that, laive with him the price of the two baistes which ye paid him, as a slight compinsation for the mintal throuble you have caused the poor fella. Then I'll forgive ye yer bargain, on condition that, as long as ye live in Dublin, ye'll never again thry to take in the poor an' the stranger, an' bring a bad name on the town!"

An' with a light heart, an' a heavy pocket, that poor man went home to his wife an' childre afther all; an' all by raison of Dan's cuteness.

But, I darsay, about the cliverest an' the long-headest thrick ever poor Dan—God be good till him!—wrought, it was on the landlord of the Head Inns in Dublin. An' it was this way.

It seems there was a poor travellin' man, a tinker be trade, goin' about, an' whatsomiver he had to do with the landlord of the Dublin Head Inns, I don't rightly know, an' can't tell for feerd to tell a lie; but anyhow the landlord of the Head Inns both chaited an' ill-thraited the poor man, an' kicked him out of his house; an' howsomdiver it was the landlord was within his rights be law—for, be the same token it's many's the wrong to the poor, the forlorn, an' the friendless that same law covers. And when the poor tinker, bein' advised by the Dublin people, went an' give in his case to Dan, Dan toul' him so in as many words.

"An' can nothing be done to the oul' curmudgeon, at all, at all?" says the tinker.

"Yis," Dan says, "something can be done, if ye put yerself in my hands."

So, off Dan takes the poor tinker, an' had him shaved an' washed, an' dhressed up in wan of his own best shoots of clothes, till he looked the very picthur of a grand gintleman, an' then, givin' him his diractions, Dan sent him off. Straight he made for the Head Inns, an' walkin' up to the counther as boul' as ye plaise, he took the landlord's curtshy, an' give him back a betther.

"Can ye commedate me with lodgin's here, landlord," says he—"bed an' boord for the next six months?" talkin' the very grandest English.

"Sartinly, we can," sez the landlord.

"I've just landed from Jarminy," sez he, "an' I called on me fren' Counsellor O'Connell, an' he recommended me here, as the best Inns in town. Now," sez he, "I want to hire yer front parlour all for meself, an' I want ye to name the tarms for the same, an' use of yer hall for me parcels an' belongin's."

"The front parlour all to yerself," sez the landlord, "'ill cost ye a gay penny, throth,—ye can't have the front parlour of the Head Inns in Dublin all to yerself for a song, an' the use of my hall for yer belongings—it'll cost ye," sez he, "let me see—I can't make it ye less nor four-an-sixpence a week, bed and boord to be exthra"—for ye know in Dublin they don't know when to stop chargin'.

Well an' good, the tarms was accepted, an' papers dhrawn up on the agreement immediately, the Counsellor himself comin' in to put his han' to the pen in witness of it. Me brave man gets in his thraps without any more delay, an' takes possession of the front parlour.

Next mornin', a'most afore the birds had begun to call, the landlord was 'wakened out of his sleep by hearin' the divil's own tindherary goin' on in the front parlour, right beneath him.

"Paddy!" he shouts to the sarvint, "Paddy! get up an' go down an' see what

The Counsellor 183

the dickens is the matther with the chap in the front parlour that he's risin' such a row at this onraisonable hour of the mornin'! Sweet sarra saize him for a vagabone! or what the divil is he battherin' at, anyhow?"

Down Paddy went, an' he wasn't there till he was back.

"Och, masther!" says he, "yon bates crayation!"

"Why? why? what the norra's the matther?"

"Och, nobbut ax me what the norra isn't the matther. It's open the door I did, an' looked in, an' there I sees me brave lad that hired yer front parlour, sittin' on the bare floore in a shoot of clothes ye wouldn't handle with a pair of tongs, a sotherin'* iron one side of him, a kit of tools the other side, as good as a barrow-load of ould sausspans an' tin-cans scatthered all over yer parlour; an' the buck himself with the anvil atween his knees, an' he hammerin' away for the bare life, puttin' a bottom in a kettle! Jeroo-salem, such a sight, masther dear! Sez I to him when I got my tongue with me, sez

* Soldering.

I: 'Me masther sends his compliments an' wants to know what are ye doin'?' 'An',' sez the lad, raichin' for a skillet to begin secondly on, an' without as much as lookin' up, sez he, 'tell yer masther that I send my compliments, an' I'm doin' what it would be fitther he was doin'—mindin' me own business.'—There's for ye, masther!"

But his masther didn't wait to hear the end of it till he was below himself, an' bouncin' intil the middle of the skillets, he lets a tearin'-ouns out of him an'—

"What? What? What's this tarnation tomfoolery about?" sez he, "in my front parlour? or what do ye mane at all, at all?"

But the lad was whistlin' like a mavis on May-day, an' timin' himself makin' a new tin on the anvil, an' the sorra a answer he made him, but went on as unconsarned as iver.

"I say, ye scoundhril ye," sez the landlord, kickin' one of the skillets clean out through the window, "get up out of that, an' clear out o' this yerself an' yer thrumpery in double quick time, afore I call in the polis, an' make them do their duty."

But the tinker got up, an' rowlin' up his sleeves, sez he,—

"Now, I'll tell ye what it is, ye oul' curmudgeon ye, get away you out of here, in double quick time, or I'll make these jintlemen"—referrin' to his fists—"do their duty; and that jintleman," sez he, plantin' his left fist under the curmudgeon's nose, "that jintleman," sez he, "is named Six-months-in-hospital; and this wan here," plantin' his right fist in the same position, "this jintleman is styled Sudden-daith. I was poor, an' lone, an' fren'less the other day," sez he, "an' ye oul' sinner ye, ye took me in, an' ye had me abused an' ill-traited bekase ye knew the law was on yer side. Now I have both fren's an' law, an' I've writin's on this room for six months to come, an' I'm detarmined to make what'll pay me boord out of it, or know the raison why. Out now, ye oul' imposther! Out o' my room, an' don't set yer dhirty foot in it, nor show yer forbiddin' countenance in it till this day six months. Out now, ye oul' speciment ye! Out!"

An' lo and behould! the next thing was,

there appears in the front parlour windy a dhirty paper settin' off,—

" To the enlightened Publick of Ireland, England, Scotland, and the Isle of Man. Old Pottes mended as good as ever, likewise repayred. Likewise Kettals, including Other Tin-cans and implements of a Like nature. Alsoe Saucepans and Frinepans. Not Forgettin' Skillets. P. S.—You can get In new bottammes while you wate. P. S.—You are requestioned to Leave All instruments for repayr in the hall. P. S. —This is the cheepest house in town for gettin' in A new bottam."

An' that was the scene it bangs me to describe! But the notice wasn't half an hour up, with the landlord goin' about through his house, up an' down, ragin' and swearin' and kicking every wan come in his way, till half Dublin was round the house, readin' the notice in the parlour windy, an' watchin' the lad tinkerin' away an' whistlin' away inside, an' wondherin' what had come over the landlord of the Dublin Head Inns to let his front parlour to a tinker. An' then again, when the customers begun to come roun'—for the Head Inns was pathronized by the Lord Mayor himself, an' all the first genthry in Dublin—when they begun to come round for their mornin' wet an' heared a tinker tinkerin' in the parlour, an' saw the hall panged up with footless pots, an' bottomless skillets, an oul' vithiran tin-cans—"Why," they says, "it's a low-come-down day with the Dublin Head Inns, when this is the thrade's goin' on in it, an' it's betther for us to push on an' find a daicent house to get a dhrink in." An' afore night there wasn't an oul' customer that hadn't disarted an' taken up their quarters elsewhere, till the landlord had to call in Counsellor O'Connell, an' by his advice go on his two bare knees to the tinker an' ax his pardon, an' his pardon over again, an' promise to behave himself in future with daicency to the sthranger an' the poor, an' give the tinker a good round penny to give up the writin's he had on the front parlour, an' clear out, himself an' his kit, which he did the very next mornin' with a fatter purse than when he went in.

That was Dan for ye!

May the soft bed, an' the sweet wan, in Paradise be his that nivir forsook the poor an' the disthressed! God Almighty rest him! an' Amen! Amen!

The Masther and the Bocca Fadh

The Masther and the Bocca Fadh*

HE was a specious villain, was the Bocca Fadh, but resourceful, tactful—clever, in the narrowest sense of the word. Ignorant though he was, a glib tongue and an audacious—almost brazen—self-confidence made him pass in the eyes of the neighbours for a sage, a long-headed fellow, a knowledgable man. He was a source of wonder—sometimes of awe—to the neighbours themselves, and a source of terror to the neighbours' childre, particularly to those of them who were attending school. "Looking for his share," as he was (though a stranger might well be surprised to see such a fine fellow, in the prime of life, looking for his living so), he put up where he list, made himself at home where he would, and by the fireside at

* Long Beggarman.

night put the youngsters "through their facin's," as he termed it—that is, when he had partaken heartily of the plentiful supper placed before him, and carefully placed his wallets and his staff in the chimney corner, and lit his pipe and crossed his legs, he condescended to inquire,—

"Well, Aillie, how is the childre advancing in their curriculum of secularity?"

"Well, musha, Jaimie" (the Bocca Fadh was Jaimie), "the norra wan of meself well knows how are they gettin' along at the larnin'—for I know that's what you mane, only you put it in a polite way—the norra one of me well knows how they do be gettin' on; but wee Gracie and Johnnie they do have the eyes sthrained out of their head o' nights, lyin' down on the h'arthstone, and thryin' to spell by the light of the *grisiog*,* an' queskinin' wan another on their books. It's often I do be tellin' them that the first night you'd be with us I'd get ye to try them to see what speed are they comin'. Maybe ye'd be so kind as to put a queskin or two on them, just to satisfy yerself, an' to satisfy me."

*Smouldering peats.

The Masther and the Bocca Fadh 193

"Yes, Aillie, I'll do that," and he looks in the direction of Gracie and Johnnie, who have now hid themselves behind their mother's skirts in mortal terror of the ordeal.

"Come out, Gracie, *a leanbh;* an' Johnnie, *a theasge*,* come out, an' go over there with yer Spellin' Book till Misther Haraghey puts queskins on yez. That's the childre—hould up yer wee heads now an' show him how much ye larned since the last time he thried yez. That's the good childre; raich him the book now."

And the Bocca Fadh takes the book from the trembling hand of little Gracie with the cynical air of one who, having taken all knowledge for his province, feels naught but the utmost repugnance to the touch of an elementary spelling-book. In one hand he takes the candle which Aillie has lighted for him, and drawing it close to the book, which is held wrong side up in the other, he dips into the book here and there, muttering "Imph!" at each dipping, with an easy nonchalance deftly turning the leaves by means of a few disengaged fingers, as one who had

* (Pron. *a haisge*) Treasure.

spent his life among books. In a short few minutes he seems to have got the gist of it, and flings the book from him with a bored air.

"Well, boy, what class are you locationed in?"

"He's axin' ye, Johnnie, dear, what class ye're in," the mother says in a deferential undertone to the dumbfounded Johnnie.

"Please, sir, in the class next the heap of thurf," Johnnie tremblingly replies.

"Imph! imph! imph!" and the Bocca Fadh stretches his legs and knocks the ashes out of his pipe as if preparing for serious work "Imph! and, my good man, can you or can your sisther consther to me,—

'*In mudeelis, in clanonis;*
In firtaris, in oaknonis' ?"*

"Oh, Misther Haraghey," the mother pleads, "but ye know they haven't raiched the Jarmin or the Latin yet. The chile's but young. If God'll spare him to us, I thrust he'll know them yet. Thry him on somethin' in the Spellin' Book."

* In mud eel is, in clay none is;
In fir tar is, in oak none is.

The Masther and the Bocca Fadh 195

"Haybrew, Aillie—that was a thrifle of Haybrew. If ye desire me to tackle him on the Jarmin, or on any other of the dead langidges, I'll be happy to obligate ye."

"Oh, no, no, Misther Haraghey, it's yourself could do that same, but just thry him on the Spellin' Book—himself and wee Gracie."

"Very well, Aillie, I'll start him a small queskin in the Coney Sections at your requist.—As I was journeyin' to Sent Ives, I met a man with seven wives, an' every wife had seven sacks; in every sack there was seven cats, an' every cat had seven kittens—now, kittens, cats, sacks, an' wives, how many went to the fair of Sent Ives? That's just a small thrifle, Aillie, to test the childre in their Coney Sections."

"Now, Johnnie, *a gradh*,"* the mother whispered, encouragingly.

"Ah, mammy," Johnnie said grievingly, "the Masther didn't put me on to Coney Sections yet—we're only at 'Stir the fire and put on more coal.'"

"Imph!" said Misther Haraghey, as he

* (Pron. *a gra*) Love.

shook his snuff-box and helped himself lavishly, without tendering a pinch to Aillie. "Let me see, now, what ye know about Bo-*tan*-ny—me good little girl,"—but his manner and tone implied, *my very bad little girl.* "Me good little girl, can you tell me whether was it Julius Cæsar or Michael Augustinian Angel-*o* that first discovered and explored the Immortality of the Soul?"

Gracie tried her very best to be brave, but the Bocca Fadh's ordnance was too heavy for her. Her under lip quickly showed signs of wavering—it trembled perceptibly, then two big tears dimmed the bright blue of her eyes; they started out—she gave way, and beat a hasty retreat behind her mother.

"*A mhilis, a mhilis!*"* said the mother, taking little Gracie in her arms and hugging her. "Whisht! whisht! *a stor:* sure Misther Haraghey wouldn't turn a hair on me own darlin's yalla head. *A leanbh, a leanbh mo chroidhe!*† don't cry like that, or what are you afeerd of at all, at all?"

"Oh, mammie, mammie, I'm afeerd of

---

* (Pron. *a villish*) My Sweet.
† (Pron. *allaniv mo chree*) Child of my heart.

The Masther and the Bocca Fadh 197

the Bocca Fadh. He doesn't give queskins like the Masther. Mammie, keep me here."

Johnnie, a better soldier, still firmly held his ground.

The Bocca Fadh looked calmly, indifferently, into the fire, and remarked to it,—

"I have only two other questions to denounciate, an' if ye answer me I'll have the shupreme sensation of awardin' yer mother's son shupairior markifications. Both queskins is in Divine-ity. Can you dimonsthrate or tell to me, me fine young man, what is the connection between the Bloody Wars an' the Comics seen in the sky—refarred to in Holy Writ, eighteenth and nineteenth of Revolutions, thirteenth chapture, nine-an'-twintieth an' following varses? Ye cannot? Well, now for the next, a simplified one. Can you prove from the canine laws of the Holy Roman Church (one Faith an' one Baptism) that the time an' times an' half a time preydicted by Columbkille for the landin' of the Spaniards at Dinnygal must occur in the present reign of the thirteenth King an' Queen of harasy in England—Victoria bein' both King and Queen—Queen of England and Emperor of Indiay?"

Brave as Johnnie was, this last assault was too much for him, he felt. So he, in turn, struck his flag and retreated rapidly also to the shelter of his mother's skirts. Johnnie did not cry; that would have been unmanly. But he could not deny to himself that he felt a curious sort of choking in the throat, which was only relieved by the gentle stroking of his white head by his mother's disengaged hand.

"Misther Haraghey," the mother said, "it's you's the long-headed man. But I'm afeerd ye're too deep for wee Johnnie an' Gracie, that hasn't got on far with their larnin' yet."

"Oh, Missis Gallagher," the Bocca, feeling disposed to be generous under the influence of Aillie's sincere compliment, said, "they're two brave smart childre, God bliss them to ye! Of course they were a wee bit nonplushed, but on the whole they've done fairly well—fairly well. I have great hopes of them, though, of course, they don't yet figure up to my iday-al. But they're only young—they're only young yet. An' to be sure, too, any little short-comin's I have exposed is more to be laid at their Masther's door than at their own. Atween yerself an' me, Missis Gallagher, my opinion of Masther Whoriskey's tutorical abilities isn't just as elevated as it might be. God knows the opportunities I got for the cultivation of my intelligence was scanty enough; but thanks be to Him for kind marcies, what little opportunities I got I made the most of, which made me the scholart ye find me—be that good, bad, or ondifferent, it's not for *me* to say."

"Well, *I* can say, what all the counthryside says, that one would walk long an' thravel far an' not meet the bate of the Bocca Fadh."

"Oh, now, ye make me blush, Missis Gallagher. Ye do indeed. I'm afeerd I must deny the allegation, it's too much entirely, too much to say of a poor, neglected, forlorn, orphan boy, that——"

"An' more nor that, Misther Haraghey, let me tell ye that the counthryside says it was a blissin' from Providence ye *didn't* get more opportunities, for they say that, like every other great jaynis that come afore ye, ye're brain would have turned with the fair *dint* of the larnin'—ye would have larned on afore ye, they say, till yer very head would burst open with it. As it is, they say, they don't know how ye stand all ye do know. There's for ye, now, if ye must know the truth of it!"

"Oh, Missis Gallagher, Missis Gallagher, this is too much entirely—too much entirely. I'll not deny, indeed, that Father Pat of the Cross-roads an' Father Edward, the curate, both give expression to themselves to the same effect a night they had me in to argue Divine-ity an' Asthronomy again' the two of them. I'll not deny it, I say, but as Father Pat said about the whiskey they told him there was no wather in, it's a resarvation of conscience with me whether I believe it or no. But as I was goin' to say, Aillie, it's my desire to come in confliction with Master Whoriskey where an' when he pleases, in the presence of witnesses, an' I won't begrudge to him all he'll be able to crow over the Bocca Fadh when he's done with him."

The Masther and the Bocca Fadh

The Bocca Fadh was sowing broadcast these indirect challenges to the Masther. Naturally, too, they were not without some effect in the country. The neighbours encountered them so frequently that a deal of fireside debating on the respective merits of the Bocca Fadh and the Masther was the natural result. The Masther himself, who at first professed to treat with the most sublime contempt " the lucubrations of that impecunious vagrant," was at length compelled to treat them seriously, and consented to meet the Bocca Fadh in intellectual combat on the Sunday night before Christmas in the Bummadier's. Over the whole countryside the news went like wildfire, causing much commotion and excited debate. Henceforward, till the great night arrived, little else was spoken of, and though it was generally believed that the Masther must score a success, there was a large and growing section who championed the Beggarman, and sturdily maintained " that the Masther would have more nor a dish to wash " ere he'd have done with his opponent. In the meantime the Masther was in a very serious mood; the Bocca Fadh in his lightest, most indifferent, most off-hand. The Masther had everything to lose; the Bocca everything to gain.

The eventful night came. The Bummadier's was more than usually packed. The Bocca Fadh, with his wallet and cudgel, occupied the corner. He was even more jaunty than usual. He held deeper subjects in reserve; told his gayest stories, cracked his driest jokes, and treated on any and every subject save the intellectual one. The Bocca had come to dinner; the Masther didn't appear till the arranged time of meeting—after night. Despite very apparent efforts to the contrary, the Masther exhibited decided tokens of nervousness in his look and manner. When he entered, a subdued and respectful murmur of salutation greeted him. To the more prominent neighbours present he nodded thanks, and took his seat in the middle of the house. Then, his opportunity being come, the Beggarman rose in his place with a stiff grace, and making a low bow to the Masther, said,—

"Benediction with thee, Masther Whoriskey, and I bid you welcome. But afther his nocturanial paramulation "—here he addressed the company—" from his residential habitation to Cornelius Higerty's abode, won't my larned friend deign to approach in more contagious proximity with the conflagration here provided for him by the luxuriant bounty of the inhabitant?"

This was the first gun from the enemy. It had been, doubtless, long loaded and primed; but with such promptitude and unexpectedness did it go off, and with such address was it delivered, that it caused more than momentary embarrassment—almost consternation—in the opposite, unalert camp.

But in a few moments the Masther had got to his feet and returned the Bocca's bow, in an infinitely more graceful and stately fashion. He said, as he approached to take the vacant seat in the opposite chimney corner,—

"To accede to the requisition of my itinerant friend, the object of our eleemosynary regards, vouchsafes me more rapturous delight than is within the circumscribed comprehension of any bifurcated individual beneath the status of a lexicographer to express."

The return fire, through delay, was not quite as damaging as it should have been. The audience mentally scored one for the Beggarman.

The brazen rascal, too, seeing the Masther's nervousness, saw therein material for unfair advantage. During the delivery of his next fire he had the cool audacity to take out his pipe, knock the ashes out of it against the chimney-brace, suck it to see if it drew well—interrupting his discourse for that purpose, and proceeded to refill it. He said, with the most villainous nonchalance,—

"Joe-ology, Al-*jay*-bra, Thrigonomethry, Fluxions, Joe-ography, Jurie's Prudence, the Confluxion of the Systems, Di-sectation, Magne-*tis*-im, Sequesthrations, Disquisitions, Mathematicians, or the Influential Carcasses*—on which of all is it your requisition and prefermentation that I should test your eruditional accomplishments, sir?"

The Beggar scored again, the scoundrel!

---

* The Beggar had evidently heard mention of the Differential Calculus.

From the shaking of heads and whispering with which this one was received around the house, there was no mistaking it.

"Sir," the Masther replied with a magnificent scorn that regained him much of his lost ground, "from my intellectual altitudes I gaze down with the most inexpressible contempt alloyed with disdainful commiseration on the pitiable aggregation and accumulation of unmitigated balderdash with which you have the audacious temerity to address me. Sir, of all subjects in the educational curriculum of this or any other country in the universe, from the Alpha to the Omega of the same, select and indicate one, and I shall instantaneously proceed to expose your unutterable ignorance to the gaze of a commiserating public."

"Very well, then, on the Confluxions of the Systems I'll take you."

"Avaunt, sirra! avaunt!" and the Masther waived his hand disdainfully.

"Having maximum magnitudes granted, how would you calculate for me the number of jags in a cart of whins* in accordance

* Furze.

with the fundamental principles of Joe-ology?"

They were coming to close quarters.

"Sir, if I buy a horse at one farthing for the first nail in his shoe, a halfpenny for the second, one penny for the third, and hence doubling till the thirty-second nail; how much will defray the gross total cost of the quadruped?"

But the Beggarman without a moment's delay came along with his answer; and it was this-wise,—

"Adduce from Harry Stotle's[*] Commentaries the proof regardin' who made Hiram's breeches."

"My peregrinating itinerant, here's one to stop your mouth:—

> *'It's down in yon meadow I tethered my ass,*
> *Where lie fruitful acres well stored with grass;*
> *How long must the cord be when—'"*

"Maybe it's on the Influential Carcasses ye'd soonest be taken. Here's at ye, then— Are you prepared to paragonically dimonsthrate to this company how many yards of

[*] Aristotle's.

The Masther and the Bocca Fadh 207

buttermilk would make a nightcap for Binban mountain?"

"'How long must the cord be when feeding all round, He won't graze less or more than two acres of ground?'

—Elucidate me that, sirra!"

"Being given the sacrificial containments," the Bocca said, by way of elucidation, "can you arrogate for my information how many faddoms of wind went through the chancel windy of Dinnygal Abbey last Janiary?"

("Faix," the breathless neighbours remarked, "the Bocca Fadh is givin' it hard to the poor Masther.")

"Sirra," the Masther said, "can you enlighten us who wrote Cæsar's Com-*ment*-aries?"

"Now for a thrifle out of Asthronomy. Taking our start from the paralysis of the hypothenuse, can you calculate, enmerate, an' dimonsthrate the number of bottles of smoke in a cart of wet turf?"

("Troth, the same Bocca has more in his head nor a comb would take out. The poor Masther's goin' to the back-han'.")

"Sir, who or what was Cornelius Nepos? and exemplify and illustrate for us the Copernican System of the Universe, and likewise say who was the probable author of the Odes of Horace (Smith's Translation)."

"I shall now proceed to take you," said the Beggarman calmly, as he wiped the stem of the pipe upon his sleeve, and tendered it across the fire to his opponent—"I shall now, I announce, proceed to take you upon Biblical Commentation an' the elements of Hydrophobia. Devolve the south an' circular sides of a three-year-old whinstone, an' proove the same by the kibe an' square roots of Joe-omethry an' Thrigonomethry."

"Sir, I hereby challenge and defy you to Square the Circle, discover the Unknown Quantity, and elucidate the theory of Perpetual Motion."

("The Masther's queskins is wonderfully clivir, no doubts, but they haven't in them the same grit's in the Bocca's.")

"Can ye say for a sartinty whom was Jinisis's* eldermost uncle on the mother's

---

* The Bocca is in all probability referring to Genesis.

The Masther and the Bocca Fadh

side, and prove the same by the totality of Fluxions?"

"Ye can't do ' *Good morrow to ye, naybour, with yer twenty geese—*'"

"A small little queskin now to testify your knowledge of horty-culture. How many steps was in Jacob's laddher, calculated according to the mean solar distance of the equinoctials?"

Yes, the Masther was no match for this charlatan—he was not possessed of enough systematic ignorance blent with a good blend of villainy.

He was somewhat tardy in coming on with his reply.

"Do you adhere to the austere doctrines promulgated by the learned Socrates, or the more sensuous ones of Epicurus? Give your reasons, and likewise state your opinion of the respective merits of Sophocles and Darius. From whom is the quotation '*a rara avis in terra*' taken, and give a literal translation?"

"Another simple one out of Genufluxions. Prove from the Scriptures, Ould an' New Testymints, that Tobias's dog had a tail, an' propound the paragorical projection of the same."

But the Masther was wiping the perspiration from his brow—the mental tension was at its utmost. He replied not. The Bocca Fadh seized the opportunity, and rising to his feet delivered himself of his carefully prepared *coup de grace.* He said, with his grandest, most rascally assumptive air,—

"Let no charlatanical fop dare dispute the atrocious voracity of my achromatical qualifications, for I am a heterogeneous cosmopolite, perambulating and differentiating intricate problematics throughout the extension of the different localities which I have mesmerized into a conglomerated catastrophe!"

And the scoundrel sat down in the lap of victory!

Father Dan and Fiddlers Four

Father Dan and Fiddlers Four

AFTER his love for God, and his love for his flock, Father Dan loved music. Good music, that is; for he confessed he never could listen to a scoundrel murdering music, but his hand would be itching to give him a dressing with his blackthorn staff.

Anyhow, once, on an old Lammas Day, there had been a wedding above in Corameen-lusk, a son of Ned Baccagh's with Winny Neil *Mhor,* and the father and mother of a good spree it was. Nothing less than four fiddlers. Three houses under the party. Whiskey *go leor,* and meat and drink to all comers. As was only to be expected, a spree on such a liberal scale had been prolonged into the next afternoon. Coming on evening the four fiddlers found themselves at the Knockagar Cross—the parting of their ways. As was also only to be expected of fiddlers coming from a feast, their manner was effusive. It was distressing to part. They alternately cuffed and kissed each other, sang and scolded. Finally, I regret to say, they were surrounded by two peelers, who in the Queen's name arrested them as disturbers of the peace of the realm, and marched them straight—or at least as straight as the peculiar circumstances would permit—to Mr. McClane's. This they accomplished by means of their clever tactical skill. For they seized upon the fiddles, not the men; and where their fiddles went there would the fiddlers follow. Arrived at Mr. McClane's, and inveigled into his office, they were arraigned and solemnly charged that they, Michael Scanlan, of Meenauish-beg, in the parish of Killymard; Thaddeus McDermott, of Meenauish-more, in the parish aforesaid, and Nail O'Byrne and Peter Throwers, both of Throwerstown, in the parish of Drimholm, and County of Donegal, were found drunk and behaving in a riotous and disorderly manner at the cross roads of Knockagar, in the parish of Inver, to the great alarm, annoyance, and distress

Father Dan and Fiddlers Four 215

of Her Gracious Majesty's most well-beloved and dutiful subjects in the townland and parish aforementioned—or words to that effect. Though the cold fact—apart from its legal aspect—was that not a lone one of the aforesaid dutiful and well-beloved subjects was alarmed, annoyed, and distressed, or would be alarmed, annoyed, and distressed, or anything but highly entertained, had the four devoted disciples of Orpheus prolonged their orgie till Christmas Day dawned on them. But law is law, and, of course, fact has got no *raison d'être* within its province.

Just then Father Dan jogged up to the magistrate's door, on Forgiveness. The name of Father Dan's old gray mare, his faithful servant, day out, day in, in fair and in foul weather, midday and midnight for close upon thirty years was Forgiveness—whereby hangeth a tale not strictly within the scope of this history. Father Dan jogged easily up on Forgiveness, and letting himself off, he entered, while Forgiveness went to graze soberly by the wayside. Going in and finding four men there arraigned, and hearing the charge, he said, "Oh! these scoundrels from Killymard and Drimholm coming into *my* parish to disgrace it and to bring a bad name on it with their drinking and their squabbling like a parcel of thravelling tinkers—ye must make an example of them, Mr. McClane—make an example of them! A month in jail with a hammer in their fist from cock-crow till bedtime will be a big help to their manners, and to the manners of every other villain of them coming into my parish for the time to come. A month in jail with hard labour and half rations—nothing less will be of any use, Mr. McClane!"

Then the spoils of war, the four fiddles, caught Father Dan's eye.

"What? Fiddles! Fiddlers? Ye butcher music, hey, do ye? Yer villainies wouldn't be complete without that."

And he insisted on each displaying his skill (or else), on his instrument. And, as it proved, they were four of as sweet fiddlers as tirrled a bow in the two baronies. And they completely *comethered* good Father Dan, whose inherent respect for good musicians asserted itself, so that he said they were good men gone wrong, gravely pointed out to them the enormity of their crime, evoked from them a hearty promise of amendment, showed Mr. McClane that, after all, he believed the nominal fine of a shilling each and costs would, on the occasion of this their first offence, appease the offended dignity of the law, out of his own pocket paid the money down on the nail, and in front of himself and Forgiveness marched them to his house, " till he'd give the creatures a pick to ate, and a wash and a brush and a heat of the fire, and put the poor fellows on their legs, and pack them for home."

And in spite of all old Kitty Byrne's grumbling—Kitty had been his housekeeper since first he had a house to keep—and Kitty was the only tyrant, other than his boy Barney, whom Father Dan feared—despite all Kitty's grumblings against the house being turned into a cow market, Father Dan insisted on their washing and brushing, and on Kitty's serving up at the kitchen-table a plentiful meal—of which, to tell truth, they were sadly in need. And despite all

Kitty's acrid personalities about making *her* house the *randyvoo* for all the thramp fiddlers and thramp fluters from end to wind of the county, with many other equally pleasant remarks, and many very dismal prophecies of where all this blather-skitin' was going to end, her four guests made a right hearty meal, for which they thanked God when they had done; and then thanked Father Dan; and finally, to Kitty's utter exasperation, thanked her—and wished her a long life and a sweet temper.

Finding they had finished their meal, Father Dan ushered them into his own little parlour, he going in front, laden with the four fiddles and with as many bitter reproaches as Kitty could contrive to pile on him ere he got all in and the door closed in the enemy's face. Then Father Dan seated the four and put his fiddle into the hands of each, and took down his own fiddle (at which he was no mean adept) from over the mantel, and proceeded to get it into tune, keenly rejoicing all the while in the prospect of a long, pleasant evening.

But it took his guests an extraordinarily

long time to tune theirs, and divers mysterious looks and winks passed between them which Father Dan was neither slow to receive nor to interpret. The short and the long of it was that the fiddlers wanted what they themselves would have styled *elbow grease,* but which in the plain man's dictionary is spelled *poteen.* Musical preparations were then temporarily suspended while Father Dan produced a quart bottle three-quarters filled, out of which after a bit of very serious and very paternal advice against the abuse of whiskey, to which the four lent a filial ear, he gave them a glass apiece, which made their eyes kindle; and they invoked blessings on his head, informed him that it put a new sowl in them, and in token thereof gave a particularly lively jig by way of flourish, the manner of which promised well for an enjoyable night.

Then Father Dan got himself seated, and all five of them gave "The Blackbird" so excellently as to draw the tears to the good man's eyes. Then there was less or more friction, for whilst Father Dan wanted some of Moore, his friends were loud for jigs and strathspeys, favourites of their own. They compromised on "An Sluadh Sidhe." When things seemed again to be going smoothly, everyone of the five putting his soul into the music, the sound of wheels was faintly heard by Father Dan; the sound ceased opposite the door; he succeeded in silencing the music in time to hear Kitty's greeting at the door responded to in the well-known voice of Dr. McGilligan, the Bishop!

Father Dan, in one awe-stricken glance, took in the room with its five fiddlers—four of them as disreputable-looking as ever sat in a priest's parlour—nursing their fiddles around a table on which was a stout quart bottle and a glass, and inwardly he asked himself why he was born! "The Bishop!" was all he could ejaculate to his startled companions. But that was enough. Quicker-witted or perhaps less frightened than he, the four musicians as with one accord popped under the table, fiddles and all; and one of them, seized with sudden presence of mind, put up a long arm from the hiding-place and bore off the bottle just one moment ere the good old Bishop, in his own familiar way,

Father Dan and Fiddlers Four

walked in unannounced. The table-cloth of generous amplitude let fall its ends to the floor around the table; and so Father Dan had half recovered himself, sufficiently recovered himself anyhow to greet his Bishop warmly, and thanked him profusely for the honour of this unexpected visit. The good Bishop instantly made himself at home, seating himself in an arm-chair to one side of the fireplace, his side to the fire and his face to the room. The sight of a glass on the table naturally turned the Doctor's discourse on the subject of all others nearest his heart, the cause of temperance. And as Father Dan, with something very much akin to twinges of conscience, gave him an encouraging account of the progress of the cause in his parish, his trial only properly commenced, for the table got a distinct knock from below, such as would be caused by the heel of an inverted bottle going up suddenly. Father Dan conjectured this was but the first of a series. And rightly. With a well prepared cough he half drowned the next rap. Proceeding with his discourse, he kept his right heel in readiness—by an opportune crack of which on the floor he confounded the following one. A shuffle of his feet fairly well confused the next succeeding one. But it was getting a trying ordeal. Adroitly punctuating his argument by a few raps of his knuckles on the table neutralized a few more. Thereat taking his cue, he became so demonstrative in his argument and clinched his points with such and so many blows on the table, that he would soon have awaked conjectures in Dr. McGilligan's mind, but that gentleman turned his face towards the fire for a moment, and the bottle, to Father Dan's utter consternation, was rapidly reached out from under the table and deposited, of all places in the world, under the heavy drapings that hung from his Lordship's chair! An old brown and bony hand, too, had gone out from under the table at a few feet distant from the rugged one that held the bottle (yet quarter-filled), and made a rather aimless grab for the bottle, and then retired slowly, as it were disappointedly, beneath the fringes of the table-cloth again. Though this proceeding took barely a few seconds, it seemed to Father Dan an hour. Distinct

Father Dan and Fiddlers Four

beads of perspiration certainly did start on his brow; he had not even presence of mind to make a noise. But as the mysterious hand missed its grab, something, which might be a grumble or might be any indistinct sound under the moon, was emitted from under the table, and the Bishop's eye, Father Dan observed, detected a swaying in the drapery depending from the table.

Father Dan said "Scat!" and stamped his foot.

"I suppose you are troubled with rats?" Dr. McGilligan said.

"Oh, yes, sometimes—sometimes—annoying villains—annoying villains. But as I was saying about Father Hugh's parish—" and he had the discourse again reverted to its proper channel, and was comparatively at ease once more.

But not for long. He observed when the Doctor looked any other way than straight before him that brown, bony, big hand came out on a rambling excursion, darting suddenly back to cover each time the Bishop's eye threatened to come back. And he then observed a bright eye glistening through a hole in the table-cloth, at about a foot from the ground. And every time the ugly hand came out, and grasped, and sprawled, he felt an itching to give it a thundering good whack of his staff that would cure it of its rambling. He had to say " Scat! " several times, when he fancied Dr. McGilligan's attention was attracted by the slight noises, or by the shaking of the table-cover. All his endeavours to entice Dr. McGilligan to be shown to his room, that he might brush himself up after his journey, were unavailing, for his Lordship would persist in having out his chat first.

The hand had come out about the tenth time, and had gone rambling and fumbling in the direction of the Bishop's chair, and had swiftly retreated on false alarms, and slowly gone forth, and rapidly come back, and hesitatingly gone pioneering again, until just as Kitty Byrne appeared with a lapful of turf for the fire, a second even uglier hand —and both were left hands—had crept out, and both were making ineffectual darts at something unseen by Kitty. She suddenly stopped short on first seeing them a few feet before her, and across her passage. Then she quickly took in half the situation: revenge was sweet, and Kitty laid down her broad and heavy boot, with very much emphasis, plump on the back of the nearest hand to her. There was a stifled cry, luckily covered by the noise with which Father Dan hitched his chair and coughed. Kitty's ankle was immediately caught firmly by a right hand, and viciously wrenched. She swayed, staggered forward, and, first her load of turf, then herself, was pitched into his Lordship's lap, out of which Kitty narrowly escaped rolling into the fire. In the commotion, *three* hands started out simultaneously from beneath the table, swooped under his Lordship's chair, the bottle rapidly passed back in one, the other two hands followed, limp, and one might easily think half disappointed. The spirit-rappings underneath the table set in again at once; sharp and quick they were. But there was yet too much commotion for them to be heard amongst the party at the fire. Father Dan sharply reprimanded Kitty for her clumsiness in tripping, and begged a thousand pardons of Dr. McGilligan, while Kitty was too much overcome with horror of the situation to do more than clasp her hands, and turn up her eyes to heaven, and cluck her tongue against the roof of her mouth, in attempted expression of her inexpressible feelings.

Good Dr. McGilligan tried to reassure and quiet them, and he repeated, "Tut! Tut! Tut!" till he got them in a moderately calm condition again. Then he consented that he would look into his room while Kitty was getting them a cup of tea. But as he would have risen from his seat, he fell back again slightly startled, for before his eyes, and apparently none interfering with it, one end of the table was suddenly tilted up some six inches, and slowly descended again. Father Dan could neither move nor speak. Kitty Byrne collapsed on the sofa. Then the other end of the table went up as mysteriously for a foot, it swayed to right and left for a few seconds, while some strange uncertain sounds were heard from beneath; then the table subsided once more, and for a momentary space there was no sound. Father Dan strove to reach for his blackthorn which rested against the wall within a yard of him—but on the way his hand was paralyzed, and fell back to his side. Now, the table bodily bounded, sharply and suddenly to the height of a foot, and as suddenly came down again. A distinct scuffling noise was heard. Then—

" Tarnation saize ye; let go me throat! "

" Let go the bottle or I'll choke ye as dhry as a whinstone rock! "

" Hish! "

" Hish, or I'll prod the ribs aff ye! "

" Let go the bottle, hatchet-face! let go the bottle! "

" Not if it was to save yer sowl, cruked mouth! "

" Ye natarnal veg ye! bad luck to ye, an' his Lordship listenin'! "

" I don't care a thraneen if Sent Pether himself was listenin', I'll have the bottle or his ribs 'ill get what Paddy gave the dhrum! "

" De'il's cure to you, spavin-feet, an' take that! "

His Lordship sat terrified. Father Dan sat terrified. Kitty Byrne lay astounded. Beneath the table then arose a general hubbub. One side the table then rose a couple of feet and sank. Then rose again—and the other side followed. Luckily, Father Dan kept his candle on the mantel. Before the startled and staring prelate the table rose up five or six feet from the ground, swayed, shook—there was a crackling noise such as might be produced by trampling on and bursting-in fiddles—and then the table shot over and lit on its side on the fender, and thence tumbled over, exposing four big fellows struggling and gasping, and punching and grappling, and finally bellowing, trampling all the while on the débris of four fiddles, to the utter and fearful consternation of good Dr. McGilligan, and the unspeakable mortification of poor Father Dan.

. . . . .

After Father Dan, with the substantial help of his staff, had cleared out the four arrant villains, and left them rubbing their wounds far from his door, and pitched out after them the sorry remains of their fiddles, he threw himself on the Bishop's mercy, explained and apologized, apologized and explained; but the Bishop, when he had gathered his meaning and purport as best he could from a disjointed statement, went into fit after fit of long, loud, and hearty laughter, which seized him at intervals even in bed that night. Father Dan affected to join, but the poor man's laugh was distressingly mechanical, and in his heart he vowed to whale and whack every fiddler from either Killymard or Drimholm whom he'd find within the bounds of his parish from that sad night forward. And certainly such were afterwards very chary of trespassing on the forbidden region.

That is the story of Father Dan and the Fiddlers Four.

Jack Who was the Ashypet

Jack Who was the Ashypet

WANST on a time when Kings and Queens was as plenty in Ireland as good people, and good people as plenty as Kings and Queens, there was a poor widdy woman and she had wan son they called Jack. Now this Jack was a lazy, good-for-nothin' sthreel of an ashypet, who sat round the fire with his heels and his toes never out of the ashes all days of the year, and all years of his life, till he grew to be man-big, and he neither good for King, country nor clippin' sheep.

Till wan day at long an' at last, he ups, and he says, says he,

"Mother," says he, "it's the black shame's on me to be hunkerin' in the ashes all days o' me life, an' you puttin' the bone through the skin thryin' to *do* for me. It has been *so* long, but it'll not be *so* longer. Bake me a bannock, cut me a callop, an' give me yer blissin' till I go away to push me fortune."

No sooner said nor done.

"Very well, Jack *ahaisge*," says the mother. And she baked him his bannock, cut him his callop, give him her blissin', an' off went poor Jack to push his fortune.

And on and on afore him Jack walked, till, in the hait of the day, haltin' to rest himself, and to eat a bit of his bannock, he observes on the flag he was goin' to seat himself down on, a flock of big black flies, an' he ups with his stick an' kilt three-an'-thirty of them,—for he counted them, an' wan o' them was a dale bigger nor the others.

"Now that's what I call a good blow," says Jack; an' gettin' an old rusty nail he wrote upon his stick—

"*With wan blow o' this stick I kilt a clargyman an' two an' thirty of a congregation.*"

Afther that, Jack he thravelled on and on, far further nor I could tell you, and twicet further nor you could tell me, till at last he come to a country where he found two Joyants buildin' a bridge. Here Jack climbs

Jack Who was the Ashypet 235

up a tree unbeknownst to the Joyants, an' takin' a wee pebble-stone out of his pocket he fires an' hits wan o' the Joyants that was in front of the other, with it.

"Don't do that again, I tell ye!" says the Joyant that was sthruck, says he, to his brother Joyant.

Then he went on with his work, but he wasn't right at it, till Jack the rascal threw another small pebble-stone an' sthruck him again.

"Be this an' be that," says the Joyant, says he, as black as thunder, "if ye do that again I'll throw ye over the bridge!"

But me brave Joyant had scarce yocked his work the second time, when Jack rattles another purty little pebble-stone off his skull.

"*Melia murther!*" roars the Joyant. An' afore givin' him time to bliss himself he had his brother Joyant be the throat an' over the bridge, an' kilt him cowl' dead on the rocks below.

An' at this me poor Jack couldn't houl' himself in no longer, but laughed an' laughed till he rowled down out of the tree.

"Oh, ye vagabone!" says the Joyant, "so

it was you that done it, an' made me kill me poor brother.—Oh ye vagabone ye!" says he, "it's me'll make the short work o' ye!"

"Stan' off, stan' off," says Jack, says he, wavin' his hand, "ye don't know who ye're talkin' to. Are you aware," says Jack, says he, "the wondherful fait that I parformed?"

"I'm not," says the Joyant, says he, "what was that?"

"I kilt," says Jack, says he, "with wan blow o' that stick, a clargyman an' his congregation of two-an'-thirty."

"I don't believe a word of it," says the Joyant.

"There, then," says Jack, handin' him the stick—"There, then," says he, "read it for yerself."

"Thrue enough," says the Joyant, his jaw dhroppin' all at wanst when he read what was on the stick. "But sure ye'll not touch me, Jack," says he, "an' I'll not say a word to ye if I had fifty-five brothers, an' ye made me kill every sowl o' them."

"Never fear," says Jack, "I have made it a rule never to intherfere with the young or the wake."

Jack Who was the Ashypet 237

So, home with him the Joyant fetched Jack; an' when Jack had got his fill of a good supper an' gone to bed, an' left the Joyant an' his oul' mother sittin' be the fire—

"Isn't this a nice how-do-you-do," says the oul' mother, says she, "that ye kilt yer poor brother all through this scoundhril's thricks."

"Oh, whisht, whisht, whisht, mother!" says the Joyant, says he, "for feerd Jack would hear ye, an' come down out o' the room an' kill us all. Whisht, whisht, whisht, mother!" says he, "ye don't know what ye're talkin' about!"

"Go to pot," says she, "for a blatherskite. I don't believe a word of it that he has the sthrength he *lets on*."*

"Oh, whisht, whisht, whisht, mother!" says the Joyant, "sure didn't me own two eyes read it off the stick!"

"Botheration take you an' the stick," says she, "for the ediot ye are! Is that all the proof ye have? I'll tell ye," says she, "what ye'll do, to thry him out for it: just

* Pretends.

ax him out to the meadow the morra-mornin' for a sthroll; I'll lave in yer way the three-ton sledge-head of yer brother's, an' the seven-ton sledge-head of yer own, an' the ten-ton wan of yer poor oul' father when he was alive: yous 'ill come across them be accident, an' you purpose to thry him a throw at them for fun. Then we'll soon see his sthren'th, an' be the garries, if he turns out the imposthure I believe him to be, we'll soon *do* for him then."

Well an' good; the mornin' come, an' me boul' Jack was up with the lark.

"What do ye say, Jack," says the Joyant, says he, "to a turn in the meadow without, to get up yer appetite?"

"I say it's no bad iday-a," says Jack.

So out the both o' them marches, Jack cheek-be-jowl with the Joyant, an' through the meadow they goes, an' it wasn't long till they come across a sledge-head.

"I say," says Jack, "what's this?"

"Oh," says the Joyant, says he, turnin' it over with his toe, "that's only a little sledge-head belongin' to me poor brother: it's lyin' here where himself an' me used to come out of a mornin' an' throw it for exercise.—What do ye say, Jack, to a throw of it?"

"Oh, of course, of course,—sartintly we'll have a throw at it be all means," says Jack.

"Will you throw first, Jack?" says the Joyant.

"Oh, not at all," says Jack, "that sort of thing would be considhered very bad manners o' me in my counthry."

So up with the sledge did the Joyant, an' at wan throw he threw it eleven mile.

"Now, Jack," says he, "it's your turn."

"Oh, just when ye threw it away," says Jack, "be good enough to lay it back again."

So, off went the Joyant an' fetched it back, an' left it down at Jack's feet.

"Himph!" says Jack, says he, lookin' at it. "What weight do ye call that?"

"Three ton," says the Joyant.

"Have ye any others?" says Jack.

"Yes," says the Joyant, says he, "there's a seven-ton wan belongin' to me, an' a ten-ton wan belongin' to me poor oul' father, lyin' about."

"Get them," says Jack.

The Joyant, all wondherment, got them.

"Get a rope an' tie the three together now," says Jack.

The Joyant done this, too; his eyes growin' bigger every minnit.

"Plaise to stand back out o' me road, now, me good fella," says Jack, sthrippin' himself of his coat, an' rowlin' up his sleeves, " an' gimme room to wind me arms, or ye might get hurted."

Back the Joyant stands, wondherin' more an' more, an' ready to dhrop with the wondher. An' Jack, puttin' his two fingers in his mouth gives a loud whistle.

"What do ye mane be that?" says the Joyant.

"Oh, nothin," says Jack, "only it's a blacksmith lives at home, an' naybours me in Dinnygal, an' when I was comin' away he put it on me if I'd meet any likely bits o' scrap-iron on me way, to be sure an' mind not to forget but pick them up an' take them home to him. But do you think," says Jack, says he, offended, "that I've got nothin' whatsomiver to do only be cadgin' bits o' scraps like these round with me? I'll pitch them home to him now an' be done with them.—That whistle's to put him on the lookout."

"Aisy, aisy," says the Joyant, "ye're not surely goin' to throw our beautiful sledge-heads home to a blacksmith for scrap-iron. *Melia murther*, no!"

"Stand back," says Jack. "Stand back," says he, making great sthrives entirely to get *by* the Joyant, an' get at the sledge-heads.

"No, no, no!" says the Joyant. "Mother, mother, mother! he's goin' to throw our purty sledge-heads home to a blacksmith for scrap-iron. No, Jack, Jack," says he, "sure ye wouldn't be as bad as that on us?"

"Arrah, bad win' to you an' yer little sledge-heads," says Jack, rowlin' down his sleeves again, an' gettin' intil his coat. "The norra be with you an' them! for to go an' for to raise such a phillalew about nothin! Take them out o' me sight," says he, turnin' an' marchin' home to his brekwuss.

An' that night again, when Jack had gone to bed, the Joyant an' his mother was bemoanin' to wan another over the fire.

"But now," says the Joyant's mother, "afther all, he didn't *throw* the sledges home.

There's no bein' up to the thricks o' them people comes from Dinnygal, an' I can't get it off me mind yet but he's maybe only an imposther. Now, we must thry him out for it; so, the morra-mornin' you put the hand-sticks in the water-barrel without, that houlds ten ton weight o' water, an' ax him help ye to carry the full of it back from the lough, an' then we'll soon see what stuff he's made of."

Right enough, in the mornin' the Joyant puts the hand-sticks into the emp'y wather-barrel, that weighed three ton weight itself, an' he says to Jack,

"Jack," says he, "me mother would like to get a dhrop o' wather fetched over from the lough beyant. This little stand only holds ten tons, an' my brother an' I used to carry her the full of it every mornin', but I know you'll be kindly enough to help me now."

"Is it help ye!" says Jack. "Oh, surely, surely, sartintly I'll help ye."

"All right," says the Joyant, "I'll take houl' o' this end of the sticks, you of that end. Are ye ready?"

Jack Who was the Ashypet 243

"Ready," says Jack. "Lift away, me jewel!"

But the minnit the Joyant lifted, Jack lets go his end, an' he brakin' his heart laughin'. "Ha! ha! ha-ha-ha-a-a!" says Jack, says he. "Do ye know what I'm laughin' at?" says he; an' he yocks to tell the Joyant a dhroll *put-out*. "Ha! ha! ha! ha! ha-a-a!" says Jack, says he, "did ye ever hear a betther wan nor that in yer born days? Ha! ha! ha! ha-a-a! what's this to do at all, at all!" says he, houldin' his sides with the laughin'. "Ha! ha! ha! ha-a-a! that's no miss of a joke," says Jack, "or did ye ever meet with the bate of it! Ha! ha! ha! Anee, anee, oh!" says Jack, says he, an' he lay down on the grass an' he rowled with the laughin'. "Ha! ha! ha! ha! ha! Anee-oh! anee-oh! anee-oh!" says he, "I'll never get over this!"

Till at long an' at last, the Joyant had to get his arms about the water-barrel an' hoise it off to the lough himself. Then, when he had it filled, he got the sticks intil it again, an' told Jack to take hold of his end, till they'd get it home.

"Yis, me fine fella," says Jack, says he, gettin' hold o' the sticks.

"Are ye ready?" says the Joyant.

"Ready!" says Jack; "lift away, me jewel!"

But the minnit the Joyant went to lift, Jack let go his end o' the sticks, nearly br'akin' the Joyant's back.

"Och, blatheration!" says Jack, as angry as ye plaise, "what's the sense o' this way o' workin', carryin' home water in wee *dhribs* like this! Tell me," says he to the Joyant, "have ye got any spades about the house? an' what size are they?"

"We have," says the Joyant, wondherin' what Jack was up to now; "there's a spade, belongin' to me poor brother that's dead, that lifts three acres at a time, an' wan belongin' to me that lifts seven acres at a time, an' wan belongin' to me poor father that lifts ten acres."

"Take an' get them three little spades," says Jack, says he, "knocked into wan middlin' spade, an' fetch it to me, an' I'll soon cut a way for the lough to get down round yer house, so that yer oul' mother 'ill only

Jack Who was the Ashypet 245

have to come to the door-step and lift whatever water she wants."

"Oh, vo! vo! vo!" says the Joyant. "Melia murther! melia murther!" says he, runnin' home to his mother an' tellin' her all how this Jack fella wanted to fetch the whole lough down round the house, so that she might fall in an' get dhrownded some mornin'.

So even the Joyant's oul' mother had to give in that Jack must be a tarrible fella, entirely, out an' out, an' they must get rid of him somehow or other.

An' that self-same night when Jack went to bed, he didn't go to bed at all, only stayed listenin' at the room door, an' heerd the Joyant an' his mother discoorsin' how they'd kill him. An' they agreed to take the ten-ton sledge-head an' go up an' kill him with it when he'd be asleep. So, me brave Jack takes a calf they had tied in the room, an' puttin' him lyin' in the bed, he put in a lot of dry sticks along with him, an' covered over the whole with the blankets, an' got undher a lump of rubbish in the corner himself.

After a while up comes the Joyant, an' he whispers "Jack!"

But the sorra answer Jack made, only snored from his corner.

"Come on, mother!" says the Joyant, goin' back to the door, "he's as sound as a top."

Up comes the mother with the ten-ton sledge-head in her arms, an' the Joyant gets behind her an' shoves her on tor'st the bed where they seen the bulk lyin'.

"Now, mother," says the Joyant, from behind her. "Now, mother," says he, "strike! an' strike hard!"

An', with that, the oul' mother ups with the sledge-head, an' fetches it down wan *sillendher* on the bulk. An' the dhry sticks cracked, an' the poor calf could only blurt out "Boo-oo-oo!"

"Ha-a-a! ye scoundhril." says the Joyant, lookin' over his mother's shoulder, "ye got that. Did ye hear his bones crackin', mother? Give him another to aise him."

So the oul' mother ups with the sledge-hammer, an' down she comes another *sil-*

Jack Who was the Ashypet 247

lendher on the bed. An' the sticks cracked again, an' the poor calf said "Boo-oo-oo!"

"Ha-a-a!" says the Joyant, "that's you, mother, give the villain wan other to aise him."

An' the oul' mother ups with the sledge-head again an' down she comes another *sillendher* on the bed.

But the poor calf said nothin' now, for he was kilt dead.

"Ah, bully are ye, mother!" says the Joyant, "now he's aised."

An' down both o' them goes to the kitchen, an' sittin' down at the fire, went out of wan fit o' laughin' intil another at how aisy they had got rid of poor Jack.

But lo! an' behoul' ye, in the middle of it all, the room-door opens, an' in steps me brave Jack into the kitchen with his shoes an' stockin's under his arm; and he dhraws forrid a sait to the fire, and sat down atwixt the Joyant an' his mother.

"Boys-a-boys!" says Jack, says he, an' him thrimblin', "I couldn't lie in that bed no longer," says he, "for a tarrible wild dhraim I'm afther havin'."

"A dhraim!" says the Joyant.

"A dhraim!" says the Joyant's mother.

"Yis, a dhraim, an' a tarrible wan entirely," says Jack. "I dhraimt," says he, that I was out in a shower o' hailstones, an' that three great, big, big wans struck me right there on the stomach, an' a'most took the breath from me. Oh, oh, oh!" says he, rubbin' his stomach hard, "I think I feel it smartin' still. Oh, oh, oh!" says he.

An' the Joyant looked at the oul' mother, an' the oul' mother looked at the Joyant; but naither o' them spoke—only shuk their heads at other, as much as to say, "There's for ye! *three big hailstones!*"

"Jack," then says the Joyant's mother, "don't ye think aren't ye a long time away from yer home an' from yer mother now? And don't ye think wouldn't it be a good notion if ye made a push back for yer own counthry *again'* mornin'?"

"It would be ill me comin' to do anything o' the sort," says Jack, "for to go for to disart ye afther all the wee kindnesses ye've shown me while I was here. No, no, no," says Jack, "you've been both mother an' father to me,

Jack Who was the Ashypet 249

an' this house is goin' to be my home, plaise Providence, for the time to come. Oh, no, no, no, don't think I'd be so small as for to go for to disart ye that way," says Jack.

So, the lee an' the long of it was that they had to offer Jack, if he'd return home, he'd have all the goold he could carry with him. An' at long an' at last Jack consented—only, he said, he wouldn't ax all the goold *he* could carry, for that would rob them entirely, out an' out; he'd only ax what goold the Joyant could carry. So, off at length the Joyant an' Jack started, an' the Joyant two-double undher a great sack of goold, an' he left Jack three days' journey on his way, puttin' him over the bordhers intil his own counthry. An' Jack soon found manes of fetchin' the goold the remaindher of the way home, where right hearty glad his poor oul' mother was to see her own Ashypet come back. But when she saw the sight o' the goold was along with him, it's sartin sure ye may be that she was beside herself with the delight. There was an open house, an' faistin', aitin', an' dhrinkin' for nine days an' nine nights—every day an' night betther nor the other an' the last day an' night the best of all.

And Jack he built a great castle with a window *again'* every day o' the year. An' himself an' his poor oul' mother lived happy iver afther.

Jack and the Lord High Mayor of Dublin

Jack and the Lord High Mayor of Dublin

In the rare ould times, long, long, ago, whin there was paice an' plinty in Irelan', an' whin you'd meet with more humours an' cracks in one day's journey than now in a year an' a day, there was an aged widdy woman, an' she had one son, an' they called him Jack. An' Jack an' his ould mother owned a wee hut of a house not a bit bigger nor that ye might put yer han' down the chimley an' take the boult off o' the door, an' they had a stretch o' land behind the house that supported one Nanny-goat in aise an' comfort. An' moreover nor the Nanny-goat, Jack owned two pet rabbits, for he had that kindly sort of a way with him, that he had a *grah* for little wee birds an' bastes, an' the little wee birds and bastes, too, was jist every bit as fond o' him. For, by the same token, Jack had a wee whistle on a runnin'-string fastened into his weskit-pocket an' buttonhole, same as you or me 'ud carry a watch an' chain, an' whin Jack would put the whistle into his mouth an' blow it, there wasn't a bird of any sort or description within a mile o' ground that wouldn't come whish! flyin' in a sthring after the other like a railway thrain, an' light all over him an' about him, waitin' to be fed, for he had them all as tame as chickens, feedin' them day an' daily from he was no height; an' they'd perch on his hands an' arms an' head, an' all roun' him, without bein' in the laste taste afeerd.

The cabin that Jack an' his ould mother lived in was built on the main road to Dublin, where, of course, there was no end of genthry an' nobility rowlin' by in their carriages day afther day as sure as ever the sun rose. An' it happened that wan day the Lord High Mayor of Dublin an' his shoot was passin' by Jack's an' his ould mother's wee hut, on his way back to Dublin from a visit he was afther payin' to a second an' third cousin of his (by his mother's side) in the Black North; an' just as he was passin'

Jack and the Lord High Mayor 255

Jack's an' his ould mother's hut what would ye have of it, but wasn't me brave Jack just at that very minnit puttin' the whistle in his mouth to call the little wee birds to their mait, an' when the Lord High Mayor he hears the whistle he ordhers the coachman to pull up, bethinkin' that it was on himself Jack was whistlin'; but there, lo and behould ye! afore ye could say "thrapsticks," there the very sky itself was a'most darkened with the dhroves of birds that come helther-skelther from all the hedges an' ditches, woods an' scrugs aroun', an' gathers roun' Jack, an' lights atop o' him, an' atop o' everything round about, some o' them even havin' the very impidence to light on the Lord High Mayor's own carriage. Faix, the Lord High Mayor he opened his eyes at this, an'—

"The top o' the mornin' to ye, Jack, me man," sez the Lord High Mayor, sez he to him, be raison there wasn't maybe a man, woman, or child in Dublin didn't know Jack like his own left han', bekase of his livin' on the main road side, that way, where they were always passin' back an' forrid.

"The tip-top o' the blissid mornin' to yerself, me Lord High Mayorship," sez he, "it's gran' yer honour's lookin' this mornin', an' might I make bould to ax afther the health o' the Missis Lord High Mayor? I hope she's purty fine," sez Jack.

"The Missis Lord High Mayor, Jack," sez he, "is as healthy as a throut, thank you. Her lungs is as sthrong as ever, an' so is her fist, an' atween yerself an' me an' the wall, Jack," sez he, "ye may thank the Lord you're not the Misther Lord High Mayor," sez he, "or you'd know that to yer cost. But about that whistle o' yours, Jack, it's a wonderful one entirely, an' I'd like to bargain with ye for it. How does it come that it has that wondherful power over the birds?"

"Och," sez Jack, sez he, seein' his opportunity o' turnin' a few pounds at the Lord High Mayor's cost. "Och," sez he, "there's a vartue in that whistle, that when I sound it there's no feathered bird of any kind within two-an'-twinty mile o' where it is sounded but must come at the call. It was a blin' beggarman," sez he, for Jack was good at makin' histhories—"it was a blin'

Jack and the Lord High Mayor 257

beggarman," sez he, "that died in me great-great-gran'father's house, an' left that whistle to me great-great-gran'father as a last bequist for lettin' him die undher their roof, an' it has been handed down from father to son since," sez he. "Och it's a wondherful great cur'osity entirely," sez Jack, "an' me father, whin he was dyin', warned me nivir to part it."

"Oh, but," says the Lord High Mayor, "ye're a poor man, Jack, an' money," sez he, "would do ye betther good any day nor the whistle. I'll give ye," sez he, "ten pounds for it."

"I'm very thankful to yer Lord High Mayorship," sez Jack, sez he, "but I wouldn't part it on no tarms."

"Come, Jack, be manly," sez the Lord High Mayor, "an' I don't care if I give ye a score o' pounds for it," sez he.

"No use, me lord," sez Jack, "I don't want to part it, an' less nor fifty pounds wouldn't purchase it."

"Done then," sez the Lord High Mayor, "I'll give ye fifty pounds for it," sez he, openin' his weskit and pullin' the purse out of the inside pocket, an' countin' down on the carraige sait two score an' ten shinin' goold sovereigns.

"There ye are now, Jack," sez he, raichin' Jack the money, "an' that's the dearest whistle," sez he, "ever I paid for."

"Ye're not half as loth to give it, let me tell you," sez Jack, "as I am to part me whistle, that has been a hair-loom in the family for up'ards of two hundred years."

So the Lord High Mayor took the whistle an' dhrove off to Dublin, chucklin' to himself at the dead chape bargain he got, an' how he fooled Jack, an' he scarce let bite or sup cross his lips when he got into Dublin till he run round all the naybours' houses showin' the whistle, an' tellin' the exthraornary great vartue of it entirely. An' the Lord High Mayor's wondherful whistle was soon the whole talk o' Dublin from one end o' the street to the other. An' then the Lord High Mayor give out a great day for showin' the merits o' the whistle, an' he hired one o' the biggest lofts in Dublin for the occasion, an' charged so much a head for gettin' in, from tuppence up, accordin' to their size an' daicency, an' every one come was to fetch their cage-birds with them—be raison there's no wild birds in Dublin to practice on. So on that day—an' a grate day entirely it was—you wouldn't think there was one, gentle or simple, in Dublin that didn't turn up there, every one with his cage over his shoulder or under his arm, an' when they were all in, an' the loft was a'most crammed full,

"Now," sez the Lord High Mayor, sez he, displayin' his whistle, "I'm goin' to show yez the exthra-or-nary powers of this wondherful little article. Yez will kindly open the windows, an' then openin' the doors of your cages," sez he, "let yer birds go free. Afther they have got time to be away a respectable distance from the house, then I'll blow this whistle, and yez 'ill behould the astonishin' sight of every mother's sowl o' them birds comin' back all together like Brown's cows, an' crowdin' in o' the windows again to yez, when they'll be every one o' them as tame as tomcats, an' yez will then kindly catch them an' put them back into yer cages again, the people with ondifferent varieties of birds takin' care not to get their naybour's bird into their cages by mistake for their own. Then yez can thank me an' go home," sez he, windin' up the norration with a great bow.

Up then went the windies, an' open flew the doors of the cages, an' out wint thrishes, blackbirds, paycocks, parrots, larks, jinny-wrans, an' canary-birds, besides siveral birds of great value an' scarcity, with no names on thim, that had come from furrin parts, an' was rackoned worth their weight in goold. Out they all flew, an' once away an' eye away, they weren't long showin' a clean pair o' heels over the roofs o' the houses, an' it was long an' many a year since such a gatherin' o' birds darkened Dublin town afore. To pass the time, then, an' give the birds time to get off far enough afore he'd call them back, the Lord High Mayor commenced crackin' jokes an' reharsin' dhroll passages that he fell in with when he was away on his visit in the North, puttin' the company into stitches laughin'—for he was a dhroll lad in his way, was the same Lord High Mayor, an' was no miss at reharsin' a story.

Jack and the Lord High Mayor 261

But well and good, the birds was long enough away at last to show the wounderful powers that he b'leeved to be in the little whistle, so puttin' the whistle up to his lips,

"Now, boys," sez he, "will yez kindly stand back a bit farther from the windies, an' give the little animals room to get in. There's a big body o' them, an' they must get a little more room nor that, or they won't be able to show in at all, at all," sez he, "stand back, boys, stand back. Policeman," sez he to a policeman was there, "do you see an' keep ordher there, and help to keep the crowd back a thrifle from the windies. That's right—that's you."

An' then he ins with the whistle into his mouth and blew a good stout, strong blow o' the whistle. "Now, boys," sez he, "now, boys, prepare an' lookout, they'll be here in a jiffey."

Then the crowd was all on their tip-toes, an' houldin' in their breaths, an' shovin' out their eyes to catch the first gleek o' the birds comin' back. They were this way for full two minnits, an' still no sign o' the birds. The Lord High Mayor himself began to look a thrifle unaisy, ye would think, an' he looked out iv the windy.

"I b'leeve, boys," sez he, "they'll be here immaidiately. It's their time now; watch hard and yez'll see them comin'."

So the boys watched harder than afore; an' they'd see things in the distance, an' say, "There they are!" "No." "What's yon now?" "It's a dhirty shirt the wind's tossin' over the house." "Here they come." "Ay, this is them." "It's a lie." "It is." "It is not." "You're a liar." "You're another." "Do ye want ye're jaw splinthered?" "There they are at last." "It's not them." "It is them." "I'll knock yer two eyes into wan." "What's yon black thing now?" "It's a lawyer's sowl that died at the town end, last night." "Hurrooh! here they are now!" "Nobbut, is it them?" "No, the divil a feather o' them yet." "They're not goin' to come at all, lads." "They are." "They're not." "Shut yer mouth, or ye won't see them if they do come." "They'll not come." "Our birds is lost, boys." "We'll nivir see the sight o' them more." "Give it up, boys, the Lord

Jack and the Lord High Mayor

Mayor has made Tom-fools o' yez." "Throth an' he'll pay for it if he has." "Ruffian!" "Villain!" "Scoundhril!"

"Aisy, aisy, lads," sez the Lord High Mayor, sez he, the colour o' the white wall wit fright—"Aisy, aisy, boys, an' I'll fetch yez back yer birds, don't fear. Just let me give one other whistle out o' the windy, an' yez'll not be able to cage them as fast as they fly in," sez he. "They mustn't have heard that last whistle I gave. But, I'll engage ye, they'll hear this one." An' puttin' his head right out o' the windy, to give the birds no excuse, he blew with a vingince.

"Now, me lads," sez he, dhrawin' himself in, "look out for yer birds."

But, *mavrone*, he might as well have told them to look out for the sky to fall, for the sorra a sign o' the birds appeared. An' then the Lord High Mayor whistled out o' every other windy o' the house, laist there should be spells on some o' them, an' then went out an' whistled at the four corners o' the house, but it was all o' no use, whatsomever. The dickens a bird or bird would come next or near him. The whole crowd b'leeved now that the Lord High Mayor had been thryin' to get up a good laugh at their expense, an' they got outragus entirely, an' small wondher.

There was naither houldin' nor tyin' o' them till they'd get at the Lord High Mayor, an' not lave two pieces o' him together, an' make him laugh at the wrong side o' his mouth. An' there was got up the greatest royot, that the likes o' it was niver seen in Dublin afore or sence, an' only for the Lord High Mayor's sojers an' polis sur-roundin' him, an' convayin' him home, batin' off the mob with their bare naked swords, there'd hev' been a story to tell that day. An' then the Lord High Mayor had to pay every man-jack that their bird went away, for his bird, an' a nice penny he was out o' his pocket when all was settled.

"Well, be this an' be that, an' be the crutch o' the cruked waiver," sez he, when all was fixed up an' blown over, "if I don't make that scoundhril Jack pay for this business I'm not the man I took meself for," sez he; an' ordherin' out a rajiment of his sojers, off he starts with them to go an' take me

Jack and the Lord High Mayor 265

brave Jack pres'ner. But, by the boots, as they come along the main road torst Jack's house, doesn't Jack eye them, an' well he knew what was up with them. So Jack had a little pet rabbit runnin' about the house, an' he sez to his ould mother: " Mother," sez he, " I notice the Lord High Mayor o' Dublin an' his sojers comin' along the road there, an' when they come this far, the Lord High Mayor 'ill come in an' ax for me. Then you're to say that I'm not at home—that I'm gone to Scotlan', but that if his business is any way purtikler ye'll soon have me here. Then ye'll catch the little rabbit," sez he, " by the ear, an' tell it to fetch Jack home from Scotlan'; give it a wee tig of a rod then that'll make it run out o' the door, an' that's all ye've got to do." Jack's ould mother promised she'd do this, an' Jack went out an' disappeared behind the house. Faix it wasn't long his shadow was aff the threshel, when who steps in as sthraight as a ribbon, an' lookin' as proud as a prence, but me Lord High Mayor, an' he sez, sez he, steppin' up the floor like a drum-major, he sez, sez he:

" I'm very desirable, madam," he sez, usin'

grate English—"I'm very desirable," he sez, "madam, to hould a few minutes' counciltation with your son Jack. Is he inside, or within?" sez he.

"My son Jack," sez Jack's ould mother, sez she, "took a run over to Scotlan' two days ago, an' isn't to be back for a week," sez she; "but if it's very great business, sure I can have him here in a couple of minutes."

"Well, I should say," sez he, "that it *is* very grate business entirely—no less than a matter of life an' death. But it puts me undher a puzzle all the same," sez he, "to know, if yer son Jack wint to Scotland, how ye could have him here in a couple of minutes."

"Faix, then," sez she, "I'll soon take ye out o' yer puzzle-atation. Jack has got a little pet rabbit here that's very convanient that way; an' no matther what quarther of the known world the man's in that ye want, even as far as Chanay or Connaught, the little rabbit will have him here in a jiffey," sez she.

An' with that, Jack's ould mother catches the rabbit by the ear an' give it to undher-

Jack and the Lord High Mayor 267

stand that she wanted it to fetch Jack out of Scotland immediately without no delay, for there was a jintleman here wantin' to see him on very purtickler business. Then, she gave the rabbit a tig of the rod, which, of course, made the rabbit bounce an' away out o' the house. Jack wasn't, maybe, more nor three sparrow-hops away from the back of the house, lying hid behind a knowe, with his belly to the sun; an' the poor rabbit, as it always did in its disthresses, made for Jack, an' Jack started up an' walks into the house, with the rabbit cantherin' at his heels. Well, my sawnies, the Lord High Mayor was more nor a bit surprised at this mericle, but he held his tongue, for he said to himself that little animal, if he only could come by him cheap enough, would be an akisition that he'd give a dale to have.

"Arrah, good mornin', me Lord High Mayor," sez Jack. "It's proud I am to see ye. How is the Missis Lord High Mayor, an' the young Lord High Mayors? Ye'll have to excuse me bein' a bit out of breath, for that rabbit took me away in a hurry, just as I was in the middle of a hearty good break-

wist in Scotlan'. What might yer Lord High Mayorship be wantin' o' me?"

So the Lord High Mayor, keepin' one eye on Jack and two on the rabbit, starts an' tells him the mess Jack landed him into regardin' the whistle, an' axed him what he'd got to say for himself, for he had the sojers just outside ready to carry him off to be hung.

"Me Lord High Mayor," sez Jack, sez he, "are ye quite positive sartain that ye said 'Whistle, whistle, do yer work, for I command ye,' three times afore ye blew—as I tould ye, when I sold ye it?"

"Go long, ye blaguard," sez he. "Ye nivir tould me nothin' of the sort, an', of course, I didn't do it."

"I nivir tould ye nothin' o' the sort!" sez Jack, all taken by surprise, if it was true for him—"I nivir tould ye nothin' o' the sort! Well, plague on me, but it's just like the misfortunate numbskull that I am, to nivir tell ye that. Och, then, when ye didn't use them words it was no more use nor a common penny whistle. Plague take me, but I'm the stupid omadhaun out an' out entirely! Any-

Jack and the Lord High Mayor 269

thing in me power I can do to recompinsate ye, me Lord High Mayor," sez Jack, sez he, "ye have only to mintion it an' it's done."

"Well, Jack," sez the Lord High Mayor, "it would be next to onpossible to recompinsate me for all the vexation, not to mintion the expince, at all, at all, that whistle cost me. Stillan'ever, I'm not disposed to be too harsh on ye, seein' ye have an' ould mother to support, so I'll only ax ye make me a present of that little rabbit ye have runnin' about there. He might come in useful to me."

"Oh, is it that little rabbit," sez Jack. "Oh, me Lord High Mayor, don't ax that. Ax anything else but that—I couldn't part that little rabbit at all, at all, he's so oncommon useful to me. Oh, ye'll have to ax some other requist—any at all undher the sun but that," sez Jack, for he seen be his eye that the Lord High Mayor had·set his heart in the rabbit. "Oh, anything at all, only that, yer Lord High Mayorship," sez Jack.

"Well," sez he, "if ye don't like to part it for nothin'—though a rajiment of rabbits wouldn't railly be enough to recompinsate me for what ye've cost me, yerself an' yer infarnal whistle—why then put a price on it," sez he.

"Well," sez Jack, sez he, "I wouldn't part with that little animal for all the goold in the King's cellars, but secin' it's yerself is in it, an' seein' that ye did lose by my little mistake in forgettin' to give ye proper diraction—seein', I say, ye did come to a loss through me, I never had it in me to see any man wronged on my account, or through any fault of mine; so, I don't care though I do lose by the transaction—just count down a hundred guineas there, an' the baste's yours."

"A hundred guineas! a hundred fiddlesticks!" sez the Lord High Mayor. "Is it a common barefaced robber ye want to make yerself?" sez he.

"Oh, all right, all right, me Lord High Mayor, there's no harm done yet—every man has his own, an' then no man's onsatisfied. I was goin' to give ye the rabbit for a hundred guineas bekase it was yerself was in it, but I'm glad ye won't take him—I'm very glad indeed ye won't take him," sez Jack, "for if I had recklessly parted with that rabbit for the money, I'd nivir regretted it but wanst, an' that would 'a' been all the days o' my life," sez he. "I'm very glad yer Lord High Mayorship didn't jump at the offer."

So, the long an' the short of it was, Jack made him believe so well that he was lettin' the rabbit go at a sackerfice, an' that he would sooner not let him go, that the Lord High Mayor at last had to count down his hundred goold guineas on the dale table to Jack; an' then takin' up the rabbit, he wint away back to Dublin again, himself an' his sojers.

Well, mavrone, it wasn't long till the Lord High Mayor had put it about all over Dublin, about the rare grate rabbit he had got entirely, an' the mortial wonderful things it was fit for, an' all Dublin was talkin' of it; an' he said to himself when they'd witness the great doin's of his rabbit, he would be well recompinsated for all the bad handlin' an' hard usage he got over the whistle. So he was detarmined to lose no time lettin' them see what he could do with his rabbit; an' as he had a brother called Jimmy that lived in Galway, an' whose birthday would come roun' in a week, he said he'd give a grate supper in the market-house, the biggest house in Dublin, on that night, an' Jimmy was to get no word of it at all, but when they'd all be ready to sit down to the supper, he'd pack off the rabbit for Jimmy an' have him there at wanst, an' that would be the surprise! So me brave Lord High Mayor went an' ordhered a supper of, oh, the very best of everything that Dublin could afford, disregardless of all expense, for that night, an' then he went roun' an' axed in all the quality, an' high-up people of Dublin to come in to the supper in honour of his brother Jimmy's birthday—nivir remarkin' at all about the way he was to fetch Jimmy there that night. An' sure enough, whin the night come, the market-house was gorjus with lights an' illuminations; an' at laist a dozen long tables was spread out, an' all the invited quality come in coaches an' carriages an' 'bushes, with at laist four black horses in ivery coach, an' great snobs of coachmen dhrivin' them with castor-hats; an' whin the parties were all gathered, they were all

Jack and the Lord High Mayor

lookin' about an' gapin' about, lookin' out to see if they'd see Jimmy, or where was he at all, at all. But sarra take the one o' them could see him, an' they were puzzled out an' out; so they called the Lord High Mayor, an' put it to him—where was Mr. Jimmy, or what had happened to him at all that he wasn't here before this?

"Oh, that's all right," sez he, smilin' a knowin' kind of a smile, an' wavin' his hand. "That's all right," sez he. "Whin the supper's ready to be sarved," sez he, "I'll soon let ye see Jimmy."

They all wondhered to themselves, what did he mean by the cur'ous smile he had on him when he said this. But they weren't long under the mistification, for, no sooner did the messenger come in to ax the Lord High Mayor that the gran' supper was ready now an' would it be sarved, when the Lord High Mayor sayed he would just sarve it immadiately, as soon as Misther Jimmy would come, an' he was goin' to send for him now. The whole company got up their ears at this, an' it sthruck them about the rabbit they had heard so much about, an' they were all on tip-toe to see the wondherful performance. Then the Lord High Mayor, he took the rabbit out of a beautiful cage he had it in, an' in the presence of the whole assembled company, he commanded it in its ear to go down to his brother Jimmy in Galway, an' fetch him here immaidiately, for that a grate supper was waitin' him. Then givin' the rabbit a tig of his walkin' stick on the behind, he made it run away out of the door.

"Now, ladies and gintlemen," sez he, turnin' to the company, "ye're about to see a very wonderful performance entirely. My brother Jimmy, as ye all know, is in Galway this night, an' doesn't know, no more than that walkin' stick of mine, about this great supper I'm getting up in his honour. But yez have all heard me puttin' the ordhers," sez he, "on that little rabbit to fetch him here; consequentially ye'll see Jimmy comin' walkin' in o' that door in an instant, with the little rabbit trottin' behin' him at his heels," sez he.

Well, of course, the whole company, all the great tip-top ladies an' jintlemen of the

Jack and the Lord High Mayor 275

town of Dublin, they were all wondherfully amazed at this. An' they were all standin' tippy-toes at once, watchin' the door to see the quare sight of Jimmy an' the rabbit comin' in, all the way from Galway. They waited this way five minutes, an' the messenger come back to ax the Lord High Mayor if he'd sarve the supper now.

"Just immaidiately — immaidiately, my man," sez he, lookin' at his watch. "Jimmy has time to be here now, an' the minute he comes you'll sarve the supper."

Still, be me song, there was no Jimmy puttin' in an appearance, an' the company had their necks strained watchin'. Afther another five minutes the man come back again to say the supper was coolin'. No odds—no supper dar' be sarved, the Lord High Mayor said, till Jimmy comes, an' he'd be here just now. But, be the toss o' war, it was plain to be seen he was gettin' a thrifle onaisy, an' when, after another quarther of an hour, the man come in an' sayed the supper was as cowld as charity, faith the Lord High Mayor he knocked him down wit' vexation, an' he started out to look for the rabbit. An' soon afther, when there was no sign of him comin' back aither, an' the supper got past takin' entirely, faix the company begun to get up their dandher wit' their stomachs achin', secin' that most of them didn't cut mait for four-an'-twinty hours afore, as they wanted to have plinty of room for the gran' supper—faix their dandher begun to get up, an' afther they passed some ugly remarks not nowise complimenthary to the Lord High Mayor, who had now made a purty fool an' town talk o' them twicet over, they started off hot foot to look for the Lord High Mayor himself, till they would taich him a lesson he wouldn't be likely to forget. But the Lord High Mayor, who was runnin' the sthreets like a lunatic axin' afther his rabbit, got word of this, an' only he raiched his own house in time, an' locked an' barred an' bolted all, an' kept within doors for betther nor a week, he'd 'a' been a sorry man, let me tell you.

But when it was all settled up again, an' the Lord High Mayor had shown how he was swindled himself, far more an' far worse

Jack and the Lord High Mayor 277

nor them, they give him pardon, an' he got free once more. An' when he was free:

"Well, be this an' be that, an' be the other thing," sez the Lord High Mayor, "if I don't make that scoundhril Jack pay for this," sez he, "it's not day yet. That's twicet the conscionless knave has robbed an' thricked me, but, by Jimminy! he'll not do it the third time. I'll ardher out me sojers," sez he, "an' I'll go to his house an' saize on him, the blaguard; an' I'll fetch him here, an' hang, an' dhraw, an' quarther him, for the addification of the Dublineers—an' that'll be the proper way to thrait the wratch," sez he.

So, ordherin' out his sojers once more, off again he started wit' them for Jack's house, determined to have Jack wit' him this time, whither or how, be hook or be crook.

As the Lord High Mayor an' his sojers come along doesn't me brave Jack again eye them, an' right well the rascal knew their arrand. So puttin' his ould mother into bed, he filled a bladdher with bullock's blood an' tied it roun' his mother's neck. Then he sat down by the hearth just to wait till they'd come. An' he wasn't long sittin' till the thramp! thramp! comes up to the main road torst Jack's house, an' in walks me Lord High Mayor up the floor, far straighter and prouder, you'd think, than ever he was.

"Arrah, begorra," sez Jack, sez he, runnin' to him with both hands out, "but it's the welcome sight for me to see yer Lord High Mayorship, an' but it's meself is both plaised an' proud to see ye; for, would ye b'lieve it, ye wcre the very idantical man I was thinkin' about—yerself an' the Missis Lord High Mayor. Sure I hope an' thrust in Providence it's right well an' hearty she is, both herself an' the young Lord High Mayors—I hope they're all as well as I'd wish them; an' may the Lord in His bounties always keep them so. Won't yer Lord High Mayorship dhraw forrid this sate to the fire, an' sit down on it, an' take a wee hate of the fire, such as it is, an' it's just poor enough—a sort of mixed, middlin', like a man comin' out o' the faver—for the thurf, thanks be to God for all his marcies, wasn't just as plentiful this year as we'd wish them. I thrust yez isn't anyway ill off for thurf in the

Jack and the Lord High Mayor 279

town now—or, sure if yer Lord High Mayorship was disthressed for a grain of thurf to make the dhrap o' tay for the Missis Lord High Mayor an' the young Lord High Mayors in the mornin', why, if you'd sen' a man out to me with a creel, I'd—I'd—I'd show him a stack where he could stale plinty."

"Will ye, for heaven's sake," sez the Lord High Mayor, " stop that tongue of yours that goes like a hand-bell. Don't give me any more o' yer palaverin', for I don't want none of it—it's too much of it, to me own loss, comes me way—I'm come here, ye notorious scoundhril ye," sez he, " with me sojers to take ye off to Dublin, where I'll hang, dhraw, an' quarther ye, for an example," sez he, commencin' an' norratin' to him all happened to him over the head o' the rabbit.

"Oh, well, me Lord High Mayor," sez Jack, " sure the divil of it is that meself an' me poor ould mother made the gran' mistake of forgettin' to give ye the wee rod we used to strike it with, for none other would do!"

"Come, come along," sez he, " ye blaguard, an' give me no more o' yer *nadiums*.

Don't think ye can take me in that way, more. Come along," sez he, "come along."

"Oh, well, if I must go," sez Jack, "I can't go away an' laive me poor sick an' helpless ould mother in bed there to parish of hunger. Betther for me *do* for her at once," sez he, takin' up a big knife, an' plungin' it down into the bed, pertendin' it was into his mother, *moryah*, but Jack knew well it was into the bladdher he put the knife, an' there, behould, up spurts the big sthraim of blood, an' more blood commenced flowin' out o' the bed an' over the floor, an' the ould mother give a groan an' stiffened out all as one she was dead.

"Och, ye natarnal murdherin' villian ye!" sez the Lord High Mayor, sez he, when he seen what Jack had done—"ye natarnal murdherin' villain ye! ye have fixed yerself now anyhow—murdherin' yer poor ould mother. Oh, ye notorious reprobate! it's burned and beheaded ye'll be now, besides bein' hanged, dhrawn, an' quarthered," sez he, "for Christian daith is too good for a ruffin of yer sort."

"Oh, aisy, me Lord High Mayor," sez Jack,

Jack and the Lord High Mayor 281

"take it aisy, man. If it matters that much about a dying ould woman that couldn't live long anyhow, sure we'll fetch her back to life again if it gives ye any plaisement."

"Go along," sez the Lord High Mayor, "ye couldn't do that."

"Couldn't I, though?" sez Jack. "We'll soon see about whether I can or no." So climbin' up to the *bak* of the roof, he takes down a cow's horn out of it, and no sooner did he blow the blast, than his mother, that was all as one as dead, jumped up in the bed, as well as ever.

"Well, that bates me!" sez the Lord High Mayor, when he saw this. "That's a most wondherful thing," sez he. "An' a most wondherful horn entirely."

"Wondherful, is it?" sez Jack. "Arrah, good luck to yer wit, if ye were livin' with meself an' me ould mother here long," sez he, "ye wouldn't make much wondher of it. There isn't that day ever the sun rises that she doesn't displaise me somehow or other, for ould people, ye know, is very cantankrus, an' there's no livin' wit' them. So, every time she puts me out in me timper it works me to kill her, an' I just stick that knife in her, an' by an' by when I cool down an' gets out o' my anger, I just take down the horn an' blow in it, an' then we live as happy as ye plaise till the nixt day. I find it very aisin' on me entirely to be able to kill her that way now an' again," sez he.

"Well, throgs," sez the Lord High Mayor, "I have an ould woman that way at home— the missis," sez he, "an' she has got her share of a tongue, an' like most women, too, she knows the use of it; and there's times that way an' I'd give a good dale to be able to take her life. An' moreover, nor that, too," sez he, "the sarvints I have got would brak the timper of a saint if it was made of wrought steel," sez he, "an' it comes over me that way, too, many's a time, to have one of their lives, an' I know it would give me grate aise to kill one o' them back an' forrid, if I could only fetch him to life again. I don't care, Jack," sez he, "if I let ye off this time with yer life, if ye give me that horn," sez he.

"Is it give ye the horn to get off?" sez Jack. "Arrah, conshumin' to me, man,"

Jack and the Lord High Mayor 283

sez he, "that horn is worth a ship's cargo of goold an' I wouldn't like to part it on no account," sez he.

But the end of it all was that after they had bargained an' banthered for lee an' for long the Lord High Mayor bought the horn off Jack for a hundred guineas. An' off he sets with the horn, himself an' the sojers, off for Dublin, as delighted as if he was made King of Irelan'. An' be me song, he was detarmined not to keep the horn long till he'd put it in use. So he went out that very night, an' carousin' till long *by* midnight, knowin' his wife would be waitin' up for him to give him a barjin with the tongue as usual. So when he raiches his own door an' raps at it, sure enough there was the Missis Lord High Mayor come to open the door, with a candle, an' as soon as she sees him she opens on him at once, and sez she:

"Ay, a nice how-do-ye-do it is, comin' staggerin' home blin' drunk," sez she, "at this time of night—or this time nixt mornin', I should say. A nice thing, indeed," sez she, "for yer poor neggar-slave of a wife to be waitin' up here this way, night an' nightly, on ye; a nice example it is, too, to the young Lord High Mayors," sez she, " an' purty boys they'll be when they get up, seein' nothin' all the days of their lives but you comin' staggerin' in as drunk as a beggar every night when they're sound asleep in their wee beds," sez she. " A purty thing, indeed."

" Will ye hould yer jaw, ma'am? " sez he.

" No, nor I won't hould me jaw," sez she.

" I warn ye it'll be betther for ye if ye do," sez he, " for if ye don't I'll soon find a way of makin' ye."

" Jist thry that for a thrick," sez she, " ye dhrunkin' scavinger ye, that's good for nothin' only *sthravagin'* the town afther night," sez she.

" Oh, ye long-tongued hussy ye! " sez he, " it's the life of a dog I haven't with ye— but I'll soon cure ye," sez he, flyin' at her with a knife that he plunged into her, an' she fell over dead with a screech that wakened the whole house, an' sarvants an' all come runnin' down to the door to see what was up, or what was the matther at all.

" Oh! " sez the first of them, when he

Jack and the Lord High Mayor 285

come down, an' seen his misthress murdhered dead—"Oh! ye black murdherer," sez he, "what's this ye have done, at all, at all!"

"Faithn, I'll soon let ye know that, me man," sez the Lord High Mayor, rushin' at him with the knife, an' leavin' him dead on the floor.

Then the nixt come an'.

"Oh, melia murther!" sez he, "what's this—what's this ye have done at all, at all, ye murtherin' villain, ye?" sez he.

"I'll show you that, too," sez the Lord High Mayor, rushing at him with the knife, an' leavin' him dead a-top of the other two.

An' every one o' them, sarvints an' family, an' all, as they comed down, they went to open on him in the same way, with a melia murther! An' every sowl o' them he left stone dead inside his hall-door.

But, my sawnies, the naybours was all awoke with the melia murtherin', an' the screechin', an' the roarin' comin' out of the Lord High Mayor's; an' they gathered about the door with the polis and the sojers, an' they saw what was up, an' they thought the Lord High Mayor was gone clean cracked altogether; an' they called on the polis an' sojers to saize him an' carry him off to be hung at once, afore he'd have time to do more harm. But—

"No, me good men, just hould on yez a bit," sez the Lord High Mayor, sez he, "an' I'll show yez somethin' 'ill open yer eyes," sez he. An' away he goes for his horn an' fetched it, an' then an' there commences to tell them all about the wondherful powers of the horn, an' that all he'd have to do would be to give one wee blast, the slightest in the worl', an' they'd all rise up as well as ever again.

The crowd looked at the horn, an' then looked from one to the other at this. An' then—

"Well, go on an' do it," sez they, "till we see."

"Yes," sez he, "but any of yez would be mindin' to get yerselves killed first, I can do it right handy an' aisy with this little knife here, an' give yez very little pain, till I fetch yez all back to life again together."

But no; they all stood back a bit from him, an' thanked him, an' said they'd not mind gettin' killed just yet till they'd see him

Jack and the Lord High Mayor 287

fetch back the detachment he had killed, back to life again first.

So seein' he couldn't persuade none of them he takes the horn, an' putting it to his mouth, he siz:

"Now, boys, stand back a bit an' give a little air, for when this crowd rises they'll be all dhrawin' in a big breath, an' they'll want all the fresh air they can."

So back they stood, an' the Lord High Mayor put his mouth to the horn, an' he blew a blast an' then stepped back to give them room to rise, but the sorra a wee finger moved in the heap.

"Eh?" sez he, "what's that? Did none o' them get up? Maybe they didn't hear it."

Some one in the crowd said he was of the same opinion that they did *not* hear it.

"Ay, that's just it," sez he, "they did *not* hear it. But they'll hear this one, or I haven't a mouth on me," sez he, puttin' the horn to his lips again, an' blowin' och! a tearin' wild blast entirely that shook the very windies in the house. But conshumin' to the one of them gave any more sign of stirrin' than if they were so many stone statieys.

"What—what's this at all, at all?" sez he. "This is a mighty quare thing, intirely."

An' so it was mighty quare, but, all he could do, an' all he could blow, if he was to blow the chist out o' himself, the sorra resaive the one o' them he could make rise, of course; for to be sure they were as dead as a nail in a coffin, an' oh! wirrasthrue! that was the play when he found what he had done, an' what that scoundhril Jack led him into once more. An' it was only the pity o' the people for him, when they heard his story, an' saw the rale grief he was in for what he had done, not mainin' no manner o' means of harm by it, that saved him from bein' strung up like a cured herrin' afore his own door. But they put pity on him, an' they let him off; an' no sooner was he off than he swore all sorts, high up an' low down, that he would never rest or get bit or sup in contintmint till he'd have Jack burned, beheaded, hung, dhrawn, an' quarthered, on Dublin sthreet, an' much grass he didn't let grow under his heels till he was on the road once more, himself an' his sojers, determined

Jack and the Lord High Mayor 289

to have Jack this time be hook or be crook, surely, an' not to be put off with no more of his palavers or his thricks, for he got enough of thim.

An', sure enough, it wasn't long till he lifts the latch on Jack's door, an' walks in, an' catches me brave Jack sittin' opposite his ould mother across the fire, the both o' thim plannin' what they'd do, or how they'd lay out the Lord High Mayor's guineas to the best advantage. But when Jack sees him steppin' in up he jumps, an'—

"*Cead mile failte* a thousand times over! an' *cead mile failte* over again!" says Jack, "but it's meself's the glad man to see yer Lord High Mayorship again. Mother, darlin', why don't ye move yerself an' wipe a chair for his Lord High Mayorship to sit down an' take a shin-hate at our little fire. Troth, it's delighted I am, if ye'd know but all. An' how, might I ax, is the Missis Lord High Mayor—may the Lord in His kindness presarve her to ye!—an' the young——"

"Come, come, ye morodin', deludhrin' rascal ye!" sez the Lord High Mayor, "I don't want no more of yer blarney, for it's too much of it, to me own loss, I got. Come along wit' me an' get into this sack here," sez he, unrowlin' a sack from undher his arm that he'd fetched special to tie up poor Jack in, so he couldn't escape—" Come along wit' me an' get into this sack, for I'm not goin' to be *done* any more be yer thricks. Every dog has his day, an' turn about, ye know, is fair play. You had your thricks, an' I'm goin' to have a wee one o' me own now. Jump in here," sez he, "for ye'll never ate the bread o' corn again."

Me poor Jack saw there was nothin' for it now only to obey, so kissin' his mother all over, an' wishing her good-bye for ever, he walked into the sack, an' they tied the mouth o' it, an' throwin' him across a horse's back set off for Dublin. But there's great depth entirely in a bottomless barrel, an' Jack had a thrick or two in his head yet. When they raiched half-ways to Dublin, the day bein' hot an' the road long, the Lord High Mayor, when he come to a shebeen by the roadside said he was blissed if he'd pass it without thryin' the quality of the poteen, for that his throat was as dhry as a lime-

Jack and the Lord High Mayor 291

burner's hat. An' the sojers was noways objectionable to taste a dhrop aither; so leavin' Jack tied up in the sack, across the horse's back, they went in an' had a caroose. As soon as me brave Jack foun' them all in he commences bemoanin' "Och, I'll not take her! I'll not take her! I'll not take her, at all, at all! Och, och, I'll not take her! I'll not take her!" When what would ye have of it but there comes by a great swell entirely, dhressed an' starched up as if he was just steppin' out of a ban-box. He comes by, an' hearin' Jack callin' out "I'll not take her! I'll not take her!" "Halloa, me good man," sez he, "what's that yer sayin', or who will ye not take?"

"Oh," sez Jack, sez he, "it's the Lord High Mayor of Dublin wit' his sojers is carryin' me off to make me marry his ouldest daughter. But for all her money an' all her family, she's not the sort o' girl for me, an' I don't want her, an' I'll not take her, but they're goin' to marry me again' me will—but I'll not have her on no account—I'll not take her! I'll not take her! I'll not take her at all, at all!" says he wit' great bemoanin'.

"I say, me good man," sez the swell, "will ye let me swap places wit' ye?" sez he.

"I will," sez Jack, "but on one account."

"What's that?" sez the swell.

"As you'll be comin' into a mortial grate fortune wit' her, I must get fifty poun' for allowin' ye to take me place," sez Jack.

"Done," sez the grate swell.

So, out he loosed Jack, and paid him down the fifty poun', and then he got in himself, an' Jack tied him up tight, an' warned him not to spake till he'd get to Dublin. He tould Jack there was no fear o' that. Then Jack wasn't well away till the Lord High Mayor an' his sojers came out o' the shebeen, an' takin' the horse by the head they started off for Dublin, an' no sooner were they there nor the Lord High Mayor ordhered a grate bonfire to be lit. An' it was lit; and all the people gathered to see the rascal Jack roastin' —for he was to be roasted half to death first. Then the sack was taken by four men an' heaved into the middle o' the flames; an' the minnit it was in, the roarin', an' the screechin', an' the squealin', an' the yellin', an' the bawlin', an' the melia murtherin' started in the sack, that ye'd think there was nine divils in it, ivery one o' them makin' more noise nor the other; an' the Lord High Mayor laughed, an' the people laughed, an' heartily enjoyed seein' poor Jack (as they thought) gettin' such a good scorchin', an' they actually danced an' whooped roun' it with delight. Whin they thought he was well enough roasted they had him pulled out, an' —och, that was the play! There the Lord High Mayor saw, an' all the people saw, it was one o' the greatest jintlemen's sons in Dublin, an' a very grate swell entirely, the greatest in the whole town, that they had roasted, an' then there was the ructions! But to make a long story short, the swell's father come, an' he wanted the Lord High Mayor arrested, and the Lord High Mayorship to be taken from him, an' it was a very narrow nick with the Lord High Mayor or he'd 'a' lost his life over it. When it was all over he shook his head an' said that rascal Jack was too many for him entirely, and he'd niver go near him more, but laive him in paice for the remaindher of his days. An' Jack an' his ould mother had plinty o' money; an' when his mother died he built a castle an' married a great lady out o' Dublin, an' lived ever afther the greatest jintleman in them parts, with a stable o' horses, an' a pack o' hounds, an' a cellar o' wine, the like o' which wasn't to be found again within the four corners of Ireland!—an' sure it was all only his disarts, for he had a cliver head, had me brave Jack.

www.ingramcontent.com/pod-product-compliance
Lightning Source LLC
Chambersburg PA
CBHW022117230426
43672CB00008B/1421